YOU'VE GOT TALENT

ANDREA MILLS

LONDON, NEW YORK,
MELBOURNE, MUNICH, AND DELHI

Senior editor Andrea Mills
Senior art editor Jacqui Swan

Managing editor Linda Esposito
Managing art editor Jim Green

Category publisher Laura Buller

DK picture researcher Rob Nunn
Production editor Clare McLean
Senior production controller Angela Graef
Jacket designer Hazel Martin
Jacket editor Matilda Gollon
Development designer Laura Brim
Senior development editor Jayne Miller
Design development manager
Sophia M Tampakopoulos Turner

Illustrators Mike Dolan,
Peter James Field, Billie Jean

Consultants Dr Andy Kempe
(Drama), Dr Peter Lovatt (Dance),
Dr Fiona Richards (Music)

First published in Great Britain in 2011 by
Dorling Kindersley Limited,
80 Strand, London WC2R 0RL

ISBN: 978-1-40536-786-8

Colour reproduction by MDP, UK
Printed and bound by Hung Hing, China

Discover more at
www.dk.com

CONTENTS

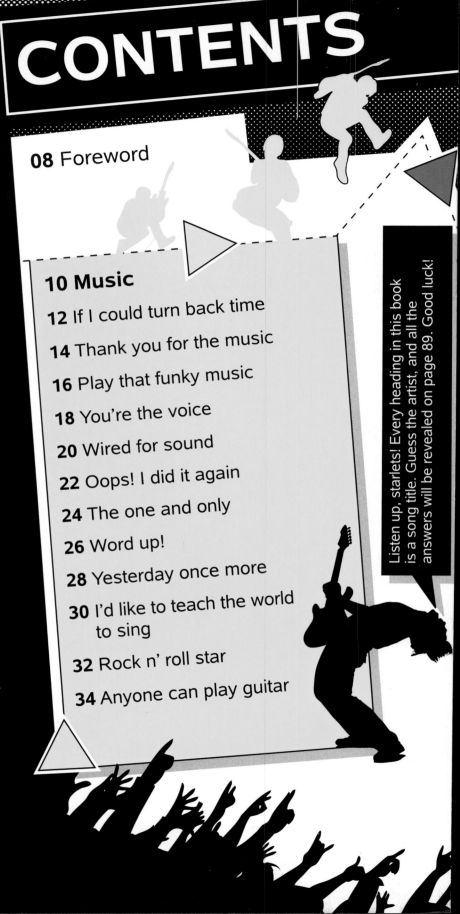

Listen up, starlets! Every heading in this book is a song title. Guess the artist, and all the answers will be revealed on page 89. Good luck!

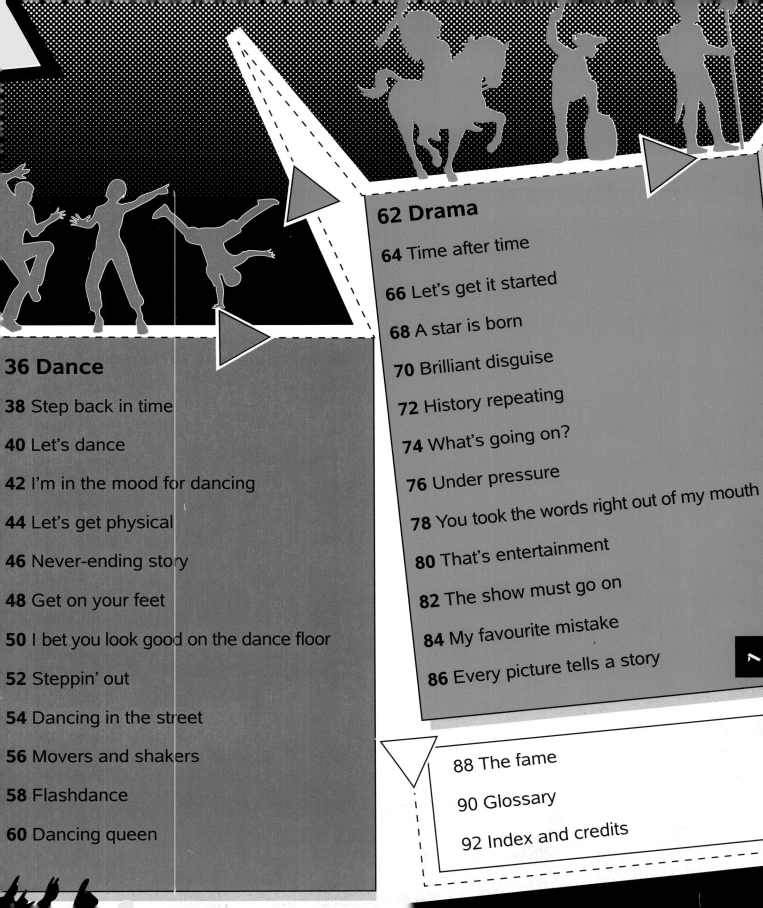

"When you believe in a thing, believe in it all the way, implicitly and unquestionable. Set your goals as early as you can and devote all your energy and talent to getting there. With enough effort, you may achieve it. Or you may find something that is even more rewarding. But in the end, no matter what the outcome, you will know you have been alive. The way to get started is to quit talking and begin doing. If you can dream it, you can do it. All your dreams can come true if you have the courage to pursue them."

Walt Disney (1901–66),
American film producer and director

MUSIC

Music is the soundtrack to our lives. Whether whistling a melody or listening to a band, hearing the dawn chorus of songbirds or the theme tune to a television programme, music has the power to affect our moods, influence our decisions, and create legends. Tune in and sing up, all you budding superstars. This is your chance to shine.

IF I COULD TURN BACK TIME

If the pop charts had existed for as long as there has been music, then there would be top-ten listings from more than 50,000 years ago! Just imagine cavemen club classics riding up the charts. Though we don't know exactly what music was like back then, it is possible to trace a timeline of history's biggest sounds and singers.

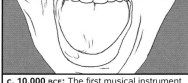

c. 50,000 BCE: The origins of music go back to when the first peoples travel from Africa to other parts of the world. As all tribes have a form of music, scientists believe that music was probably invented in Africa.

c. 10,000 BCE: The first musical instrument is the human voice, used for all forms of expression. The first true musical instrument is probably made from animal bone.

c. 3,000 BCE: The first known music in a written form is in ancient cuneiform on stone tablets in Sumeria (a country of southern Mesopotamia in what is now Iraq).

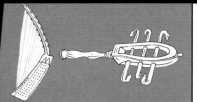

c. 2,000 BCE: Ancient Egyptians are big music fans, especially as music is associated with the gods they worship. They play harps, flutes, and sistrums (sliding rattles).

800 BCE: The Ancient Greeks also play some of the first instruments, preferring early versions of bagpipes and double pipes. In the popular epic poems of the time, the *Iliad* and the *Odyssey*, the words are sung aloud and played on musical instruments as the listeners dance.

c. 500 BCE: Mathematician Pythagoras (570–475 BCE) finds that the pitch of a musical note produced by a stretched string relates to the string's length.

c. 250 BCE: Invented in Greece, the first organ uses water power to blow air through a series of pipes when the organ keys are pressed. It is called the hydraulis. Electric fans do the job today.

c. 600 CE: Islamic music becomes popular. The Persian and Arabian caliphs (spiritual heads of Islam) enjoy listening to singers and musicans who play the two-stringed tanbur.

700 CE: Music takes off in China, as new orchestras form with more than 100 musicians. The first musical academy in China is established, called the Liyuan, or Pear Garden. It is founded during the Tang dynasty by Emperor Xuanzong (685–762 CE).

1030: An Italian monk named Guido of Arezzo devises a system for learning music by ear. Today, voice students still use the system of solfège to help them remember their vocal exercises.

c. 1180: During the Middle Ages, wandering troubadours sing songs of love while playing the viol or harp as they travel around Europe.

c. 1430–1600: The Renaissance (French for "rebirth") period sees an expansion from strict religious music to more varied composition played on the lute and sung by groups of musicians.

c. 16th century: A string instrument called the vihuela becomes much more popular than the lute and early guitar. Over time, the guitar evolves into its present form and becomes the world's most popular instrument.

1550: String instruments develop into the forms we recognize today. The main makers of these instruments are based in Cremona, Italy.

1590: Musicians gather in Florence, Italy, to talk about the prospect of music drama. The result is the introduction of opera. In 1598, the first Italian opera is produced – *Dafne* by Jacopo Peri (1561–1633).

1637: As opera proves to be a hit, the first public opera house opens in Venice, Italy. King Louis XIV (1638–1715) has his very own grand opera house in Versailles, France.

c. 1700: The piano is invented by Italian Bartolomeo Cristofori (1655–1731). Over time, families gather around pianos for a sing-song before radios and gramophones are invented.

1725: Italian composer Antonio Vivaldi (1678–1741) writes his famous piece *The Four Seasons*. In total, he produces more than 400 concertos, 75 sonatas, 40 operas, and 23 symphonies.

1742: German-born composer George Handel (1685–1759) performs his popular *Messiah* in Dublin, Ireland. When Handel moves to London, he writes *Water Music* for a royal boat trip on the River Thames.

1770s: Austrian composer Wolfgang Amadeus Mozart (1756–91) starts young. At the age of six, he is already known as a composer and pianist. He writes 41 symphonies and 22 operas before his death aged just 35.

1827: Thousands of people line the streets of Vienna, Austria, to show their respect at the funeral of celebrated German composer Ludwig van Beethoven (1770–1827).

1846: Belgian inventor Adolphe Sax (1814–94) creates the saxophone for use by military bands. It is later used widely in pop and jazz music.

1877: The ballet *Swan Lake* is first performed. During this Romantic period, music sounds more emotional, reflected in works by composers such as Tchaikovsky (1840–93), Verdi (1813–1901), and Wagner (1813–83).

1877: American inventor Thomas Edison (1847–1931) invents the first piece of recording equipment, the phonograph, which resembles an early record player.

Late 1880s: Named after its "ragged" rhythm, ragtime music becomes popular. It starts in the USA and is usually played on a piano.

1904: The London Symphony Orchestra is established, with the first concert played on 9 June. It becomes one of the world's most famous orchestras.

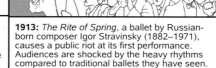

1913: *The Rite of Spring*, a ballet by Russian-born composer Igor Stravinsky (1882–1971), causes a public riot at its first performance. Audiences are shocked by the heavy rhythms compared to traditional ballets they have seen.

1917: Small groups of musicians gather in New Orleans, USA, to form the first jazz bands. The Original Dixieland Jazz Band makes the first commercial jazz recording.

1932: The first electric guitars are produced to amplify sound. Initially used by jazz musicians, they are now most popular with rock stars.

1935: American jazz singer Ella Fitzgerald (1917–86) fronts the Chick Webb band and quickly establishes herself as an international solo artist.

1939: Indian musician Ravi Shankar (1920–) begins his career playing the sitar. He becomes a huge star, later working with The Beatles.

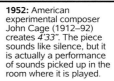

1948: The long-playing vinyl record is introduced by American label Columbia Records. A year later, 45 rpm vinyl records are sold by RCA Victor in the USA. The format is very popular.

1952: American experimental composer John Cage (1912–92) creates *4'33"*. The piece sounds like silence, but it is actually a performance of sounds picked up in the room where it is played.

1956: Snake-hipped singer Elvis Presley (1935–77) emerges as one of the world's first rock stars with his debut single, *Heartbreak hotel*. Many more hits follow, as he becomes a music legend.

1957: *West Side Story*, a romantic musical by American Leonard Bernstein (1918–90), is shown in the USA.

1958: *Billboard* debuts its Hot 100 music chart. The track *Poor little fool* by American singer Ricky Nelson (1940–85) is the first number one on the chart.

1961: Italian tenor Luciano Pavarotti (1935–2007) makes his operatic debut. He later sings *Nessun Dorma* ("None shall sleep") at the 1990 World Cup.

1963: Liverpool pop group The Beatles become huge. The term *Beatlemania* describes their fans' manic reaction to them.

1979: The world's first portable stereo, the Walkman, arrives on the market. It is designed to listen to prerecorded cassettes while on the move, and quickly becomes a fashion accessory for young people.

1981: The American television channel MTV launches, showing music videos all day and night. The first video to be shown is *Video killed the radio star* by British band The Buggles.

1983: The first compact disc (CD) is manufactured by record labels Sony and Philips. By the late 1980s, vinyl records are in decline as CDs are mass-produced.

1982: King of pop Michael Jackson (1958–2009) releases *Thriller*, which becomes the biggest-selling album in history. The zombie video for the title track becomes instantly recognizable.

1984: Leading pop artists unite under the name Band Aid to release *Do they know it's Christmas?*, with proceeds going to help famine victims in Africa.

1990s: Girl power takes over the world! English pop band the Spice Girls become the biggest-selling girl group of all time, while American pop star Madonna continues to dominate the charts.

1997: MP3 players go on sale to the delight of music fans everywhere. Thousands of tunes can now be downloaded onto this new format. Software on the Internet lets people share their music online. Instead of buying CDs in stores, people can choose to download singles and albums as a speedier and cheaper option. The popularity of MP3 leads it to become the must-have item for the 21st century.

2000s: Television programmes, such as *X Factor*, *Pop Idol*, *America's Got Talent*, and *Britain's Got Talent*, become popular around the world. Ordinary people are turned into huge singing stars, such as Leona Lewis in the UK and Kelly Clarkson in the USA.

The future: The current stream of new singing stars who entertain the younger generation is sure to continue. New genres may emerge as music keeps developing around the world. The evolution of music technology may mean one day we are all recording our singing efforts at home on the latest format for the masses to hear. As English singer John Miles put it, "Music was my first love and it will be my last, music of the future and music of the past." And who can argue with him?

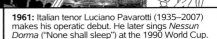

THANK YOU FOR THE MUSIC

Music is ultimately indefinable. So many different genres and styles exist around the world that it is difficult to squeeze all the varieties into only a few words. However, while genres overlap, spread out, and mix with other styles to produce new sounds, there are some core categories that remain rock steady. Let the music play to decide which ones are music to your ears.

JAZZ

Jazz started in the USA during the late 19th century, when parts of European music were combined with the rhythmic harmonies brought over by African slaves in the south of the country. This style of music has a strong and lively beat, with jazz musicians often improvising (making up the music as they play) in either solo or group performances.

CLASSICAL

The array of musical styles that were originally written to be played at churches, concert venues, or theatres comes under the umbrella term *classical*. Composers may write their music for a full symphony orchestra or just a small choir of singers. People are still hooked on classics today. The great composers, including Bach (1685–1750), Vivaldi (1678–1741), and Beethoven (1770–1827), are popular many centuries after their music was first written.

ROCK

Causing a stir when it first hit the American music scene in the 1940s and 1950s, rock n' roll featured energetic vocals, strong beats, and powerful melodies. Electric guitars, bass guitars, and drums became synonymous with the distinctive sound. As the hair grew longer and the hits got louder, rock music emerged. From soft rock to heavy metal, the genre encompassed a range of exciting styles that continue to be popular today. Grab your guitar and hairspray, and get rocking!

RHYTHM AND BLUES

This popular form of music was first developed by African-Americans in the USA during the 1940s. Drawing on elements of blues and jazz, Rhythm and blues (now nicknamed R&B) has evolved to include other styles, more closely linked with disco and dance. Today's stars of R&B are known for their smooth melodies and strong vocals, such as Usher and Alicia Keys.

WORLD

Although this genre sounds like it has gone global, the term *world music* is used to describe non-Western music – in particular, the sounds of Africa and Asia. The traditional music of local cultures can still be heard today, such as Indian raga music, Japanese koto music, Tibetan chants, and the Balkans' village music. Indigenous peoples take pride in keeping their own unique styles of music alive.

POP

This one's for all you pop pickers. If you follow the music charts and buy the latest releases, you're sure to be a fan of this modern genre. Pop is simple in structure and strong in melody. This winning combination usually results in songs that stick in the memory. Thanks to mass production and promotion, pop is a commerical force to be reckoned with. Today's singing superstars become known quickly to audiences around the world. While some artists on the pop scene turn out to be one-hit wonders, others prove a hit for decades, such as Madonna and Michael Jackson.

COUNTRY

The roots of country music grew from traditional folk sounds of the southern and western USA, which were known for their basic melodies, heartfelt lyrics, and acoustic guitars. Country music has blossomed into one of the world's best-selling genres, with stars, such as Taylor Swift, enjoying big sales and tours.

> *"Music is a world within itself, with a language we all understand."*
>
> Stevie Wonder (1950–),
> American singer and songwriter

RAP

The streets of New York spoke volumes in the 1970s when this African-American form of music took off. Black and Hispanic performers made up rhyming lyrics to chant over a musical melody, though sometimes they didn't use any music at all. Samples of other artists' tracks and the sound of vinyl records being scratched are other sure-fire indications that it's a rap! Performers also use the latest conversational vocabulary to relate to their audience, and keep things bang up to date.

DANCE

Disco inferno! This genre of music took European and American nightclubs by storm during the 1970s. Repetitive, rhythmic beats ensured the floors were filled with dancing queens and disco divas. As synthesizers (keyboards that could alter sounds) became popular, dance found its own distinctive electronic sound. Using turntables to mix live dance music, DJs were thrust into the spotlight, too. Famous in their own right, they were sure to get the party started.

Budding musos, gather around. If you're thinking of taking up an instrument, know your options. You may enjoy a toot on the flute or a tinkle on the ivories, but consider carefully what would make you a true music maestro. There is a wide range of instruments to choose from. Some people start small with a recorder or flute, while others go supersize on the cello or piano. Here's a guide to start you making sweet music.

small piccolos and flutes playing high notes, through mid-range oboes and clarinets – then deeper and down to the big boys, bassoons and contrabassoons.

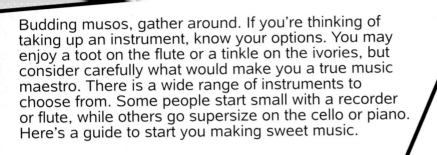

BRASS

Everyone will hear you coming if you go for the brassy option. The way to produce sound on a brass instrument is to blow air through the mouthpiece into a hollow brass tube. The note is changed by pressing down on different valves lining the exterior of the brass tube. With instruments such as trumpets, tubas, and French horns in the brass family, you'll be blown away by the choices. Ensure you have plenty of puff, though, as this one could leave you breathless!

"It's easy to play any musical instrument: all you have to do is touch the right key at the right time and the instrument will play itself."

J S Bach (1685–1750),
German composer

TOP TIPS

- Think about the musical styles that you enjoy listening to and then choose an instrument to suit them. Rockers might opt for the guitar, classical enthusiasts could prefer the violin, and jazz fans may try the trumpet.
- Instruments can be expensive, so shop around and make sure you try before you buy.
- Be realistic about where you live and where you're going to be practising your instrument. If you live in a flat, a piano may be too large and an electric guitar may be too loud!

PIANO

Have you got perfect pianist fingers? Long, slim fingers are just the job, but if yours are more like a bunch of bananas, this instrument could be a no-no. All pianos consist of an iron frame on which metal strings are tightly stretched. Pressing the piano keys makes hammers hit the strings, which then vibrate. The soundboard under the strings resonates and the different notes are heard. The two types of piano are upright and grand. Upright pianos are most common, while grand refers to both the size and sound.

SOLO

In terms of practice and performance with your chosen instrument, you could steal the show by going solo. Daily practice at home could turn you into a brilliant musician. If you can learn to read music as well, you will give yourself the benefit of playing existing music and the opportunity to create your own songs. One-on-one classes with a music tutor are another great way to learn from experience and develop your expertise.

STRINGS

Take your pick from the variety of string instruments that make up the string family – guitars, violins, violas, cellos, and harps. The largest of the string section is the double bass, which also plays the lowest notes. While all the string instruments of an orchestra have four strings, the guitar has six. Beating them all is the modern concert harp, which has either 46 or 47 strings, as well as pedals for the feet.

ORCHESTRA

If you have opted for a string instrument, you could join a string quartet to practise. This is a group of four musicians, comprised of two violins, a viola, and a cello. Over time, if you become skilled at either a string, brass, woodwind, or percussion instrument, you could become part of an orchestra. This large group of instrumental musicians is kept in time by a conductor who stands at the front.

PERCUSSION

If you can easily pick up a rhythm, percussion instruments might be the best way forward. Masters of the beat must choose between instruments that can be tuned to different musical notes, such as xylophones and glockenspiels, and those that cannot, such as cymbals, gongs, rattles, and triangles. Though hitting these instruments harder results in louder sounds, playing percussion requires a very precise amount of force to make sure each vibration results in a perfect sound.

BAND

Wannabe rock gods may prefer to join a band. Music groups are usually made up of a drummer, at least two guitarists, and a lead singer. A band can give you more freedom to play your own music and experiment with different styles than the more structured ordering of an orchestra.

YOU'RE THE VOICE

Ever heard your favourite artist belt out a tune and thought, I could do that? Artists at the top of their game make it sound easy, but in reality, effort is required to sound pitch perfect. Warming up first is crucial to preserving a healthy singing voice. Perfecting your breathing and posture are also important, while singing exercises will help to improve your vocals. Soon, you'll be singing like a star.

WARM UP

Without a good warm up, you run the risk of damaging your vocal chords, and then you'll never win the *X Factor*. It's safety first for most singers, who start by warming up their bodies with some very light physical exercises. This ensures there is minimal muscular tension in the body, so the singing voice does not come across as strained or tense. In addition, these exercises can kick-start deep breathing, which also helps to support your voice.

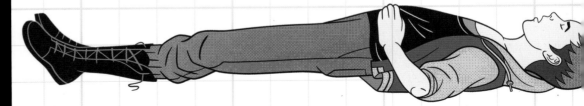

Lie flat on your back and put your hands on your waist, with fingers pointing towards the belly button.

BREATHE BETTER

Good breathing goes hand in hand with strong singing. To work out if you are breathing in the best way, place your hand on your belly button. This area should expand first as you breathe in and spread until your chest is expanded. Make sure you don't lift your shoulders or push your stomach out. It is most important that you breathe from your diaphragm, not your lungs. This is because you need to control the air that you're breathing out as you sing, and breathing from the diaphragm gives you a lot more air to work with. Focus on filling up your stomach from the bottom to the top with one deep breath. Do not fill yourself to bursting, but inhale just enough air so that you can feel the difference between a shallow breath taken when breathing from the chest. If you feel you are not breathing properly, practise the exercise shown here until you are breathing naturally from the abdomen. Once you have mastered this exercise, repeat it ten times every morning and evening.

Take a very slow, deep breath.

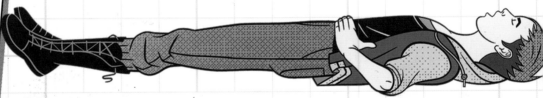

Feel your stomach and hands rise gently upwards and outwards until your chest starts to expand. Breathe out slowly.

STAND CORRECTLY

Now you've got abdominal breathing in the bag, take a good look at how you stand. Perfecting your posture will help you to deliver the strongest vocal performance. Stand up and face forward. Keep your shoulders sloping and relaxed. Place your feet shoulder width apart. Point your toes forward, with your weight balanced evenly between your heels and soles. Keep your knees slack. Ensure the front of your neck is left loose – you must never stretch it. Relax your face and jaw. Your whole body should feel comfortable and relaxed. Even if you feel nervous, ensure no part of your body is reflecting that with any tension.

Do

Re

Mi

Fa

So

La

Ti

Do

Start by standing tall, with your knees loose and toes facing forwards.

SING SCALES

Another basic exercise to improve your singing style is to practise scales. Try using solfège, in which each individual sound is pronounced Do-Re-Mi-Fa-So-La-Ti-Do, or give singing the vowels (A-E-I-O-U) a go. The recommended time for practising scales is about 30 minutes a day.

Hold your head up and keep your chin level.

Sing, superstar!

TOP TIPS

- Watch your diet. What you eat and drink matters. Dairy products, especially milk, cause mucus to build up in the throat, which restricts the impact of your voice.
- Listen to the lyrics and feel the music. Sing songs that are special to you, as this will make for a more powerful performance. Play original versions of songs to hear whether you are in tune.
- Make recordings of your voice, so you can listen to your vocal problems and start to improve them.

WIRED FOR SOUND

Technology has transformed the way we listen to music. Where once bulky record players ruled the roost in the home, today's smooth operators enjoy the benefits of portable, lightweight MP3 players. While a record player could play only one song or album at a time, an MP3 lets you choose from thousands of tunes at once. The digital revolution has given music fans more options than ever before.

RECORD PLAYERS

Also known as phonographs, record players kept music spinning around from the late 19th century onwards. The arrival of the 45 rpm single in 1949 proved popular with young people who enjoyed buying the latest tracks and playing them time and time again. However, repeated playing resulted in scratched records, which proved less of a hit. Together with records losing their sound quality over time, there was room for improvement in the music market.

CASSETTE PLAYERS

Formats first began to get smaller when cassettes reduced records onto tape (magnetic film). Cassettes were inserted into players, with half an album on one side of a tape and the second half on the other. Cassingles (tapes of single songs) soon followed, though whole albums remained the most popular. They were easier to store than records, though sound quality deteriorated over time and the cassette tape could also spool out inside the player.

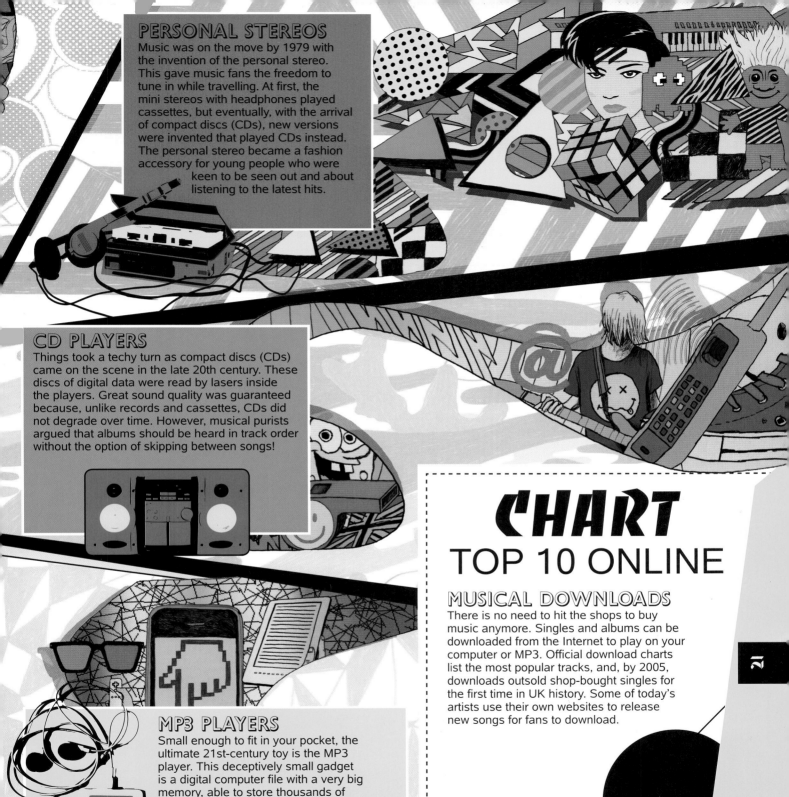

PERSONAL STEREOS

Music was on the move by 1979 with the invention of the personal stereo. This gave music fans the freedom to tune in while travelling. At first, the mini stereos with headphones played cassettes, but eventually, with the arrival of compact discs (CDs), new versions were invented that played CDs instead. The personal stereo became a fashion accessory for young people who were keen to be seen out and about listening to the latest hits.

CD PLAYERS

Things took a techy turn as compact discs (CDs) came on the scene in the late 20th century. These discs of digital data were read by lasers inside the players. Great sound quality was guaranteed because, unlike records and cassettes, CDs did not degrade over time. However, musical purists argued that albums should be heard in track order without the option of skipping between songs!

MP3 PLAYERS

Small enough to fit in your pocket, the ultimate 21st-century toy is the MP3 player. This deceptively small gadget is a digital computer file with a very big memory, able to store thousands of songs and videos that the user can scroll through and select from at the touch of a screen. As MP3s evolve, there are even more functions to choose from, including surfing the Internet.

CHART
TOP 10 ONLINE

MUSICAL DOWNLOADS

There is no need to hit the shops to buy music anymore. Singles and albums can be downloaded from the Internet to play on your computer or MP3. Official download charts list the most popular tracks, and, by 2005, downloads outsold shop-bought singles for the first time in UK history. Some of today's artists use their own websites to release new songs for fans to download.

MUSIC

OOPS! I DID IT AGAIN

It's bad enough when you trip up or make a fashion no-no in everyday life. Now, just imagine if your embarrassing or unexpected moment was seen by thousands of people all over the world. Music history is full of mistakes and mishaps, courtesy of pop's finest. Turn a healthy shade of pink on their behalf as you relive them again. Start squirming...

ALL SHOOK UP

Singing sensation Elvis Presley (1935–77) must have considered checking in at Heartbreak Hotel after his dance moves went unappreciated by television cameras in 1956. His jerky gyrations were considered so shockingly saucy that he was filmed only from the waist up for the duration of his performance. What a wasted effort!

SMELLS LIKE TEEN SPIRIT

"Here we are now, entertain us," requested grunge kings Nirvana during the 1990s. In reality, they were providing all the entertainment that was needed. During the MTV Video Music Awards in 1993, bass player Krist Novoselic kept with rock n' roll tradition by throwing his guitar up in the air to catch it. Unfortunately, he broke with tradition when it landed on his head! He then had to leave the stage for treatment.

ELECTRICAL STORM

Many people speculate as to how rock dinosaurs the Rolling Stones are still playing after all these years. Guitarist Keith Richards is definitely lucky to be alive after an incident in Sacramento, California, in 1965. As his guitar strings touched a live microphone, Richards suffered a huge electric shock that knocked him over with the force. Medical experts believe it was only the rubber soles of his Hush Puppies that saved him from certain death.

WE'LL MEAT AGAIN

Lady Gaga's wardrobe is always an eye opener, but few could keep a poker face when they saw her outfit at the MTV Video Music Awards in 2010. Wearing a dress made entirely of red meat, she was definitely a cut above the rest! However, plenty of people had a beef about it afterwards, and the paparazzi ensured her photograph was everywhere alongside the critics' comments. Lady Gaga bagged herself eight awards on the night, though the dress itself left with nothing.

"I've been imitated so well I've heard people copy my mistakes."

Jimi Hendrix (1942–70), American guitarist and singer

BAT OUT OF HELL

When a toy was thrown on stage at a concert in Iowa, USA, in 1982, Ozzy Osbourne didn't bat an eyelid. He'd seen it all before. His fans regularly threw rubber toys and raw meat in his direction. This time it was a bat. The Prince of Darkness picked it up and bit the head off, assuming it was made of rubber. Not a good move. It was a real bat! Osbourne had to go to hospital immediately for jabs to prevent him contracting rabies.

PRETTY IN PINK

Fiesty American popstrel Pink gave fans more than they bargained for at her concert in Nuremberg, Germany, in 2010. Attached to a wire meant to fly her over the audience, she ended up crash-landing into the crowd when the wire failed to connect properly. That must have got the party started!

FREE BIRD

In 2010, at an outdoor concert in St Louis, USA, rock group Kings of Leon were showered with more than just the audience's praise. Birds of a feather stick together and one local flock of pigeons did just this, as they flew overhead and showed their appreciation by covering the four-piece in a splattering of poo. The audience must have felt they had a bum deal when the band gave up and left the stage, presumably to have a shower!

LIGHT MY FIRE

American superstar Michael Jackson (1958–2009) had a hair-raising experience while filming a television commerical for Pepsi in 1984. Singing away to hit single *Billie Jean*, he was unaware that sparks from fireworks going off behind him had set light to his hair. To the relief of thousands of fans watching the sizzling spectacle, the flames were fanned, and the King of Pop kept his hair on.

BITTERSWEET SYMPHONY

For their PopMart tour of 1997, Irish legends U2 got the shows underway by arriving on stage from inside a giant lemon. At the date in Oslo, Norway, things turned sour when the fruity route failed. U2 were left in a bit of a squeeze, as the lemon stayed firmly shut. Finally forced to climb out of the back and make a more ordinary entrance, the band must have felt a right bunch of lemons.

CANDYMAN

Fans of British singer David Bowie may try to keep him sweet, but well-intentioned gifts have not always been well received. In 2004, at a concert in Norway, a lollipop was thrown to the Starman on stage. Of all places to land, it lodged in Bowie's eyelid! Ouch. There was no lasting damage, but he must have kept his eyes peeled on stage ever since. No more eye candy, thank you!

MUSIC

THE ONE AND ONLY

Recognize this lot? Probably not! With careers spanning weeks, not decades, it's safe to say there are no real superstars here. Forget music legends. One-hit wonders is where it's at. These pop pickers didn't trouble the charts for long – in fact, blink and you missed them! So let's take a trip down memory lane to see some of music's most bizarre and brief chart offerings.

TOP TIPS

- Avoid novelty or Christmas-release debut singles. Though they drum up sales and interest at the time, your name may only ever be associated with that song.
- Don't pair up with something furry! Avoid the Muppets or any other children's character for your first release to ensure you earn respect as an artist.
- Have a selection of strong tracks ready for release, so your follow-up single is not considered a huge disappointment by comparison.
- Don't fall victim to overexposure. Choose publicity opportunities carefully so you remain interesting.

SEVEN WONDERS

It can be difficult to find true one-hit wonders. Many artists you might presume to have had only one hit actually released follow-up singles that failed to chart very high. Other artists that sank without trace in one country then went on to have successful careers in other countries. Here are seven of the greatest one-hit wonders from around the world. Note that many of them are novelty singles with comedy lyrics, suggesting that the artists were not always planning a long, serious career in music anyway.

THE BIG BOPPER *CHANTILLY LACE* (1958, AMERICA)

Nicknamed The Big Bopper, larger-than-life American singer Jiles Perry Richardson (1930–59), shown right, was best known for this catchy tune. Unfortunately, his career was cut short when he died in a plane crash.

CARL DOUGLAS & VIVIAN HAWKE *KUNG FU FIGHTING* (1974, JAMAICA)

Just in time for the karate-film craze of the 1970s, this duo went to number one on both sides of the Atlantic with their tongue-in-cheek effort.

JOE DOLCE *SHADDUP YOU FACE* (1980, AUSTRALIA)

This novelty song from Down Under was released by American-born, Australia-raised Joe Dolce (1947–). It sold more than six million copies around the world. Not bad for a satirical song about Italians!

THE VAPORS *TURNING JAPANESE* (1980, UK)

Although this song told the story of a doomed romance, the quirky and memorable chorus resulted in a huge hit for British pop band The Vapors. They even enjoyed minor chart success in Japan!

NENA *99 LUFTBALLONS* (1984, GERMANY)

German songstress Nena (1960–) went to number one in her native country with this catchy number. The song was later re-recorded in English as *99 red balloons* and re-released, becoming a hit all over again.

DESIRELESS *VOYAGE VOYAGE* (1986, FRANCE)

Taking Europe and Asia by storm, French singer Desireless (1952–) found a chart winner in *Voyage voyage*. The synthesizer pop track sold more than five million copies.

LOS DEL RÍO *MACARENA* (1995, SPAIN)

Spanish duo Los del Río devised this famous dance song about a woman named Macarena. The accompanying dance routine in the music video led to people copying the steps.

ANIMAL MAGIC

Sometimes, all you have to do is throw an animal into the mix to warm the hearts of softies everywhere. Popular puppet and cartoon characters from children's television programmes can be the ideal front for a hit single. Their cute or comedy voices over the music add to the appeal. While children enjoy hearing their television favourites perform in the singing stakes, adults are also often amused by them.

SYLVESTER & TWEETY PIE
I TAWT I TAW A PUDDY CAT (1951)
A Warner Brothers favourite, this song continued the love-hate relationship between sly Sylvester the cat and calm canary Tweety Pie, using the characters' voices from the cartoons.

BANANA SPLITS
THE TRA LA LA SONG (1968)
Not actually a bunch of bananas in perfect harmony, but a dog, gorilla, lion, and elephant from the popular children's programme singing a song so catchy that it is hard to shake from your head.

ROBIN THE FROG (KERMIT'S NEPHEW)
HALFWAY DOWN THE STAIRS (1977)
Imagine Kermit but smaller and sweeter. His nephew, Robin, broke hearts when he sang (gribbited?) this simple song from the comfort of his staircase. Guaranteed to leave a frog in your throat.

TELETUBBIES
TELETUBBIES SAY EH-OH (1997)
Animal, mineral, or vegetable? It's hard to know which category the Teletubbies fall into. Whatever they are, the fab four hit the high notes with this nonsensical offering.

CRAZY FROG
AXEL F (2003)
Despite irritating ears up and down the land, computer-animated Crazy Frog leapt up the charts. He pushed his luck with a follow-up single, before hopping back to oblivion.

SCREEN HITS

A successful film, television series, or commercial can lead to a theme tune being released as a single. It's not a sure-fire road to success, but it certainly doesn't hurt. Previously unknown artists can find a captive audience for the first time by recording a theme for something that will be played and promoted to a mass market. The danger is that the artist then becomes so linked to the product or programme that it is difficult for them to break new ground after.

THE MASH SUICIDE IS PAINLESS
(1980, THEME FROM *M*A*S*H*)
This film and television series from the 1970s featured fictional characters working in a hospital during the Korean War. The theme tune belatedly became a hit after receiving a lot of radio airplay.

VANGELIS CHARIOTS OF FIRE
(1982, THEME FROM *CHARIOTS OF FIRE*)
The memorable scene of athletes running along a beach in the British film *Chariots of Fire* was accompanied by dramatic instrumental music. The now iconic piece is played at sporting events around the world.

ROBIN BECK *FIRST TIME*
(1988, RECORDED FOR A COCA-COLA COMMERCIAL)
This sugary-sweet power ballad about young love was the perfect choice to advertise the famous fizzy drink. American singer Robin Beck (1954–) found fame and the number-one spot when the song was later released.

PARTNERS IN KRYME *TURTLE POWER*
(1990, THEME FROM *TEENAGE MUTANT NINJA TURTLES*)
It was all about trendy turtles with eye masks and attitude when this American hip-hop song was released to coincide with the film. Duo Partners in Kryme failed to achieve the same success following this hit.

THE REMBRANDTS *I'LL BE THERE FOR YOU*
(1995, THEME FROM *FRIENDS*)
The phenomenally successful American television series *Friends* resulted in a big hit for the show's upbeat theme tune.

> *"It's all fleeting. As fame is fleeting, so are all the trappings of fame fleeting. The money, the clothes, the furniture."*
>
> Johnny Cash (1932–2003), American singer and songwriter

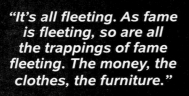

HOW TO:

WORD UP!

It's only words, and words are all a lyricist has to produce the best song around. Whether you're scribbling a heartfelt ballad or packing a punch with a credible rap, here's a guide to getting started. Songs can bring people's moods up or down, and stay in the memory forever. It is the skill of the songwriter that creates these powerful feelings, and now it's your turn.

26

THINK UP LYRICS

Consider first whether you want to write about a general subject, such as travel or history, or about a subject that's personal to you, such as a friendship or a happy memory. If you don't want to write about something specific, you can try following your stream of consciousness to see what comes out. Nailing one verse and the chorus is a great start to building the rest of the song. As the chorus is repeated throughout, this clear structure helps with the flow of the remaining verses. Don't worry about writing lines of even length or making them all rhyme. Neither of these things are essential in songwriting, but if you want to make the lines neat and the words rhyme, you can always do this at the end once you are happy with the overall content.

Grab a pad and pen, and fill it with words or phrases you like. Even doodle some pictures of what you would like to convey in the song.

Consider your audience. Who are you writing for? Ensure that your words will appeal to a broad range of people.

Try to avoid clichés about falling in love and broken hearts. This has been done so many times before that you will sound unoriginal and boring.

Obvious rhyming words such as *love* and *dove* sound too contrived, so only go for rhymes that feel natural.

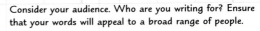

Hear the melody in your head. Either hum it into a tape recorder or play it on an instrument. Be sure you capture it, so you don't forget it. Make sure it is original and not a homage to another song's melody that you like listening to!

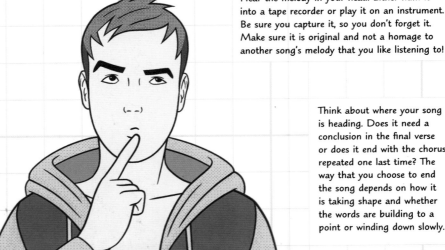

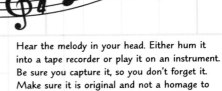

Think about where your song is heading. Does it need a conclusion in the final verse or does it end with the chorus repeated one last time? The way that you choose to end the song depends on how it is taking shape and whether the words are building to a point or winding down slowly.

TAILOR WRITING

If you are writing your song from scratch without any music to base it on, think about the music genre that your song might suit. Laid-back and relaxing lyrics probably wouldn't suit a dance track, for example. Similarly, an upbeat, uptempo lyric may lose some of its lively impact if played by a solo pianist. Even if you cannot play an instrument yourself, you need to work out how you want your words to be sung and to what style of music.

WRITE TO MUSIC

If you are lucky enough to be a member of a band or you already have a piece of music ready made for you, this can be an easier way to write song lyrics. With the luxury of being able to listen repeatedly to the music, you can sit back and consider how it makes you feel. As the music puts you in a certain mood, you'll be ready to start writing lyrics to suit it. You also have the advantage of being able to sing your lyrics over the music to hear how it sounds.

"Each song has its own secret that's different from another song, and each has its own life. Sometimes it has to be teased out, whereas other times it might come fast."

Mark Knopfler (1949–),
British singer and guitarist

RAP IT UP

Budding rappers should follow these recommendations:
- Familiarize yourself with different kinds of rhymes and ways to rap, so you are aware of all your options.
- Rappers like to stay a step ahead of the competition, so keep up to date with current words in wider use and include them in your rap lyrics.
- Practise by learning some of your favourite raps off by heart and have a go at them yourself.
- Record yourself rapping to improve the timing and flow of your words.
- Unlike other types of song, raps do not have to be written down first. Freestyling over a backing track can produce some of the best results.

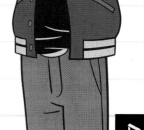

BRING ON A BALLAD

Sensitive souls should try these tactics if they want to produce the best ballad:
- Listen to ballads that float your boat. What is it about them that really pulls on your heartstrings? Once you have worked out what affects you emotionally, you are in a better position to try to do the same with your ballad.
- Most ballads follow this formula – verse, chorus, verse, chorus, climax, instrumental section, and chorus. Ballads usually start off slow and work up to a crescendo, so bear in mind that your ballad should be building to a climax both musically and lyrically.
- Ballads usually share some set features. These include verses of four lines each, heavy repetition, and a narrative in the first person to increase the level of emotion. Sob!

TOP TIPS

- Flick through newspapers, search the Internet, and listen to people for lyrical inspiration. A great line or phrase may be all you need to start a song.
- Rewrite your lyrics. Most lyricists need to play with their songs a bit to make them perfect, so revisit them again.
- Record yourself singing the song to hear how strong the lyrics sound.
- Many best-selling songs are successful because the chorus has a strong hook that draws the listener in. If you find a catchy chorus, you may have a hit!

YESTERDAY ONCE MORE

Look at the charts and listen to the radio – history's hits are making a comeback. Blasts from the past continue to be revived by today's leading artists. As classic tracks are given a different spin, a new generation of young pop pickers get to hear songs for the very first time. What goes around comes around, but what will come around next?

COVER ME

When a singer or band re-records an existing song, it is called a cover version. Although some artists stay true to the original, the current trend is to give it more of a twist. Not only can the lyrics be sung in a completely different way, but the music genre and speed may change, too. Some songs become more popular as cover versions than when they were first recorded. However, certain songs are so good that they are considered untouchable, which can lead to a backlash of criticism if an artist tries to cover it.

> *"There are only so many notes. What makes something original is how you put it together."*
>
> Lenny Kravitz (1964–),
> American singer and guitarist

SINGING SHOWS

Competitive singing on television programmes is all the rage. Shows such as *X Factor* and *Pop Idol* invite members of the public to try to become singing stars. They go through a demanding audition process including boot camp and performances on live shows. Most of the entrants cover existing songs from the past 50 years that escaped the young audience the first time around. Celebrity judges give their opinions and the viewing public vote for their favourite singers. The eventual winner is given a recording contract and releases a single soon after.

JOIN THE CLUB

It is not only reality competitions that have made singing so popular today. Fictional television shows that depict talented youngsters who dream of stardom also attract a massive following. In the hit American musical series *Glee*, a school club give its unique take on established songs, bringing them to a new audience. The blend of enthusiastic vocal performances and high-energy dance routines inspire young viewers to follow in their fancy footsteps.

MAGIC MEDLEYS

Some songs are musical "mash-ups" of a variety of established hits. Lyrics from one song are taken and combined with others to form a new single. As lines from different songs merge together, the resulting combination of lyrics may have an entirely new meaning. These medleys can breathe new life into classic tracks and appeal to a young audience who are not familiar with each of the originals. For example, the soundtrack to the film *Moulin Rouge!* (2001) featured Nicole Kidman and Ewan McGregor duetting on a long medley that sampled songs from The Beatles, U2, David Bowie, Joe Cocker, and Elton John.

RECENT REVIVALS

Some cover versions find a new audience a long time later to enjoy a classic track, such as Madonna's version of Don McLean's *American pie*, the Pet Shop Boys' rendition of Elvis Presley's *Always on my mind*, the Glee cast's take on Journey's *Don't stop believing*, and *X Factor* winner Alexandra Burke's interpretation of Leonard Cohen's *Hallelujah*. Occasionally, a contemporary hit is covered as well. Rihanna's smash hit single *Umbrella* was number one in 2007, but already there have been multiple covers by artists such as McFly, Manic Street Preachers, JLS, and Jamie Cullum.

TOP TIPS

- Don't cover a song that has been done to death. The public will have grown tired of hearing it, so be original when taking your pick. Try to find a little-known number that no one else has re-released as a hit single. Make it a song that you enjoy, but may not be widely recognizable to the mass market.
- Consider how to bring something new to the song, so you have a clear reason to cover it.

I'D LIKE TO TEACH THE WORLD TO SING

If you think you've got what it takes to be a champion crooner, test yourself. Don't be the great pretender miming into your hairbrush to Beyoncé or Justin Timberlake. Lip-synching is for losers. The best way to sing is to burst into song, whether in the shower, on the way to school, or just hanging out at the weekend. Sing solos to family and friends, and definitely give karaoke a go. Practice is your springboard to singing success.

"You're gonna have to learn to get out there in front of those cameras and hold your head up. Take charge when you're singing."

Patsy Cline (1932–63), American singer

KARAOKE CRAZE

Meaning "empty orchestra", karaoke was first heard in 1971 when Japanese drummer Daisuke Inoue invented the interactive music machine. Once a song was selected from the machine's long list, the music played without the original lead vocal, while lyrics appeared on screen for the user to follow and sing into the accompanying microphone. Inoue didn't patent his invention, though, missing out on a small fortune as karaoke grew in popularity. The craze was big in Japan during the 1980s, before spreading around the world. Everyone who ever dreamed of singing could now give it a go by performing in crowded bars and restaurants. Today, there are karaoke parties, rooms, and machines for hire, as well as in-house karaoke machines for families to sing together at home. The *X Factor* and *Pop Idol* are also essentially giant karaoke competitions in which the entrants showcase their voices by performing old hits. Altogether now, *"I did it myyyy way!"*

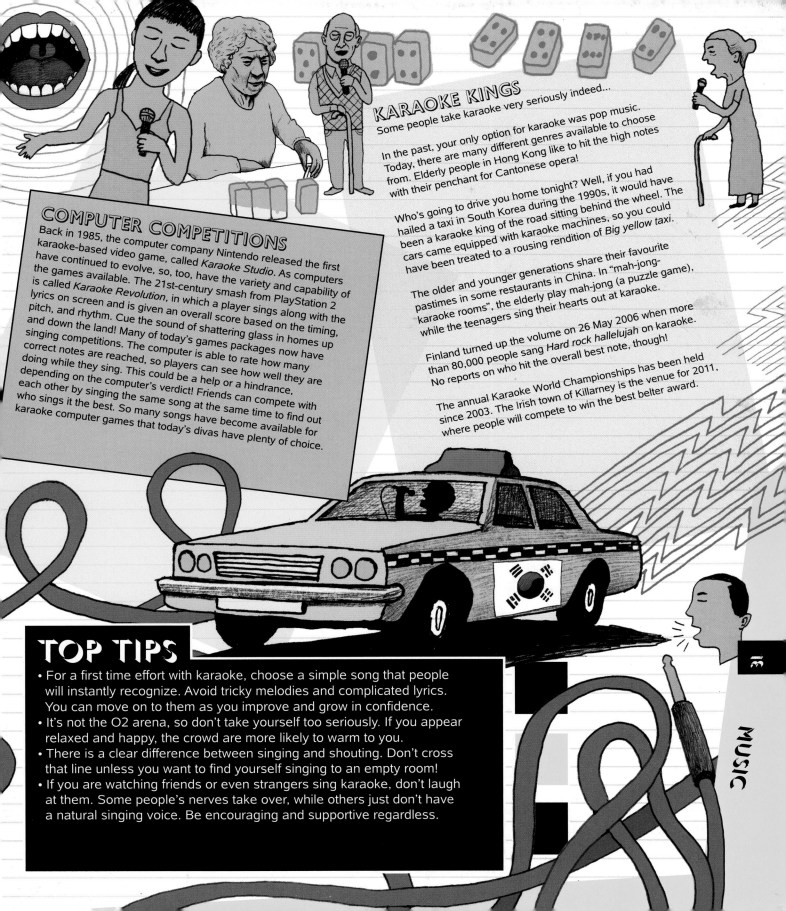

KARAOKE KINGS

Some people take karaoke very seriously indeed...

In the past, your only option for karaoke was pop music. Today, there are many different genres available to choose from. Elderly people in Hong Kong like to hit the high notes with their penchant for Cantonese opera!

Who's going to drive you home tonight? Well, if you had hailed a taxi in South Korea during the 1990s, it would have been a karaoke king of the road sitting behind the wheel. The cars came equipped with karaoke machines, so you could have been treated to a rousing rendition of *Big yellow taxi*.

The older and younger generations share their favourite pastimes in some restaurants in China. In "mah-jong-karaoke rooms", the elderly play mah-jong (a puzzle game), while the teenagers sing their hearts out at karaoke.

Finland turned up the volume on 26 May 2006 when more than 80,000 people sang *Hard rock hallelujah* on karaoke. No reports on who hit the overall best note, though!

The annual Karaoke World Championships has been held since 2003. The Irish town of Killarney is the venue for 2011, where people will compete to win the best belter award.

COMPUTER COMPETITIONS

Back in 1985, the computer company Nintendo released the first karaoke-based video game, called *Karaoke Studio*. As computers have continued to evolve, so, too, have the variety and capability of the games available. The 21st-century smash from PlayStation 2 is called *Karaoke Revolution*, in which a player sings along with the lyrics on screen and is given an overall score based on the timing, pitch, and rhythm. Cue the sound of shattering glass in homes up and down the land! Many of today's games packages now have singing competitions. The computer is able to rate how many correct notes are reached, so players can see how well they are doing while they sing. This could be a help or a hindrance, depending on the computer's verdict! Friends can compete with each other by singing the same song at the same time to find out who sings it the best. So many songs have become available for karaoke computer games that today's divas have plenty of choice.

TOP TIPS

- For a first time effort with karaoke, choose a simple song that people will instantly recognize. Avoid tricky melodies and complicated lyrics. You can move on to them as you improve and grow in confidence.
- It's not the O2 arena, so don't take yourself too seriously. If you appear relaxed and happy, the crowd are more likely to warm to you.
- There is a clear difference between singing and shouting. Don't cross that line unless you want to find yourself singing to an empty room!
- If you are watching friends or even strangers sing karaoke, don't laugh at them. Some people's nerves take over, while others just don't have a natural singing voice. Be encouraging and supportive regardless.

MUSIC

ROCK N' ROLL STAR

Welcome to your crash course in coolness. If you turn into a rock n' roll star by the end of it, you'll have made the grade. It's not enough to have a good voice and some great tunes. We're looking for star quality. To stand out from the crowd and become the stuff of legends, head straight to your first class. Don't run in the corridor, though. Rock stars never rush. Just keep it casual, giving only the merest hint of superstar.

NAME GAME

Whether you're a solo artist or part of a band, make sure you choose the right name. If you've been given a less than star-spangled effort, don't be afraid to change it to add some sparkle. Go for something out of the ordinary, so your new name sticks in people's minds. Lots of stars do it. Check out the legends below who didn't stick with the names they were given at birth. Would any of them have had the same success if they had stuck with their real names? Hmmm, it makes you wonder.

- Bono from U2 – formerly Paul Hewson
- Boy George – formerly George O'Dowd
- Cliff Richard – formerly Harry Webb
- Elton John – formerly Reginald Dwight
- Tina Turner – formerly Anna Mae Bullock
- Stevie Wonder – formerly Steveland Judkins
- Sting – formerly Gordon Sumner

ROCK ON

Once you've mastered an instrument or your voice is ready for lead vocals, it's time you formed or joined a band. Then, when you've got an exciting selection of songs together and you've recorded them so you know how they sound, hire a music studio for a couple of hours where you can lay down your tracks on CD. If that's too pricey, don't worry. Just record yourself at home and keep re-recording until the sound is how you want it to be. Get your mates around to have a listen. In the past, it was usual to send your recording off to record labels. Now it's much easier to get yourself heard. You can upload your demos to websites such as YouTube or Myspace where anyone can log on and listen to your music. You could also set up your own website advertising your music and watch the hits stack up! It's a good idea to arrange a local gig to showcase your tunes. The more people hear you, the more word will spread. Keep the faith. Not everyone is an overnight success, so be patient.

> *"If you're looking for youth, you're looking for longevity, just take a dose of rock n' roll. It keeps you going. Rock n' roll is good for the soul, for the well being, for the psyche, for your everything."*
>
> *Hank Ballard (1927–2003), American singer*

FAN CLUB

Develop your fan base as much as possible. Whether in school or in town, hand out flyers about your music, including where it can be heard on the Internet, as well as a list of future gigs to drum up a buzz about yourself. Create a website where you can upload pictures and include a news section that you can update for your fans. Online blogs are also a hot topic for starlets. Celebrities compile personal journals for the Internet so their fans can follow their movements. Be interesting and witty in your blog. Sound busy even if you're not. Talk about your plans, but don't overdo it. Even your die-hard fans don't care what your cat wants for Christmas, so spare them too much detail or you'll end up sounding boring and self-indulgent.

CHANGE OF IMAGE

Image is everything. If you wear that jumper your mum bought for your birthday, forget having a number-one record. Think about what your favourite rock stars wear. Buy some style magazines to give you ideas. Look in second-hand shops for vintage bargains. Get a second opinion – do you suit slick and smart or untidy and understated? Find the style that works for you and stick with it. But not permanently. To be a lasting icon, you need to keep reworking and updating your style to keep the audience's interest. Madonna is a classic case. Over the decades, she has adopted different hairstyles, outfits, and musical approaches. Despite having a short career by the Material Girl's standards, Lady Gaga continues to change her look with outrageous costumes and props that leave her fans gaga for more. No shrinking violets allowed. Sticking a telephone on your head and carrying a teacup 24/7 may seem extreme, but it's a small price to pay for star status.

CROWD-PLEASER

It doesn't matter whether you're headlining Glastonbury or performing at a party, if there's an opportunity to work the crowd, make the most of it. Don't look blown away by the size of your audience, though. Own the stage and give off the vibe that this happens all the time. Enjoy brief interactions with the audience between songs, but keep it all about the music. Don't forget the encore. Pretend the show's over, then come back and do another track, so you can revel in the cheering crowd, but always leave them wanting more. Singing or playing guitar are not your only options. Hungarian composer Franz Liszt (1811–86) was a huge star in the 19th century, playing sell-out piano recitals, so don't restrict yourself. Just play whatever music appeals to you.

TOP TIPS

- Keep up to date with current trends and fashionable bands on the music scene. If your finger is on the pulse, you can lead the competition, instead of following it.
- Be mysterious. If you reveal all about yourself, people will lose interest. With your air of mystery, people keep talking and your star shines ever brighter.
- Don't assume superstardom comes only with rock n' roll. There are examples of legends in classical music, such as violinist Nigel Kennedy, so if that's where your talent lies, go for it.

HOW TO:

- NUMBER STRINGS
- HOLD THE GUITAR
- POSITION FINGERS
- PLAY CHORDS

ANYONE CAN PLAY GUITAR

The most iconic instrument for rock stars is the guitar. It's easy to see the appeal when you watch your heroes. Electric guitarists can steal the show at live concerts with their fast fingers and sensational solos. If you want to join them up on stage, don't expect to be Jimi Hendrix overnight. It takes focus and practice to hit the big time. But once you get the hang of it, expect to raise the roof with the noise!

NUMBER STRINGS

Let's start with the basics. A guitar has six wire strings that are plucked to produce musical notes. The thickest string is on the top, with the thinnest string nearest the bottom. These strings are numbered in order from the highest-sounding pitch (the first string, so number one), down to the lowest-sounding pitch (the sixth string, so number six). Each string is also identified with a letter from the musical alphabet. String 1 is E, string 2 is B, string 3 is G, string 4 is D, string 5 is A, and string 6 is E. Knowing the letters helps you when you are reading music. As you recognize the letters, you will know which strings you need to play.

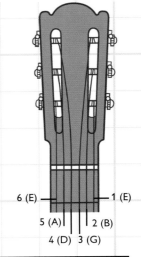

6 (E) — — 1 (E)

5 (A) — — 2 (B)

4 (D) 3 (G)

HOLD THE GUITAR

If you are right-handed, take the neck of the guitar in your left hand so that the back of the guitar is flat against your body. Support the neck of the guitar with the thumb of your left hand so that your fingers are ready to play the frets (raised bars on the fingerboard). Plucking one string produces a musical note. Plucking while holding the string down above one of the frets results in a different note. Your left hand holds down the strings over the frets to make the variety of notes, while your right hand is used to strum the six different strings.

BODY

FINGERBOARD

FRETS

TUNING PEGS

NECK   NUT   HEAD

BRIDGE SADDLE

SOUND-BOARD

SIDE

SOUND HOLE

TOP TIPS

- Keep practising the chords, so you don't need to follow the graph diagrams and you can play them without having to think where to put your fingers each time.
- Don't start playing songs until you are confident that your chords are perfect. This ensures that you are clear in your mind about chords, so your eventual song playing comes easily and naturally.
- You can make up melodies using the chords that you are learning. Even though there are famous songs that use the chords you have learned, you don't have to stick with them. Plus, you might end up with a new hit on your hands!

34

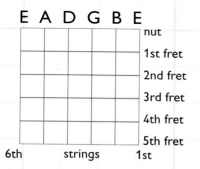

E A D G B E

nut
1st fret
2nd fret
3rd fret
4th fret
5th fret

6th   strings   1st

coloured circles show you which fret and string to pluck

1

numbers in coloured circles show the finger to use for the fret

POSITION FINGERS

In guitar music, the four fingers of the hand holding the guitar's neck are numbered as follows – 1 is your forefinger, 2 is your middle finger, 3 is your ring finger, and 4 is your little finger. The graph (shown left) is a representation of the guitar. The vertical lines represent the six strings, while the horizontal lines represent the five frets on the guitar neck, except for the top line, which is the guitar nut. Circles are marked on this chart to show how a piece of music should be played, including the frets and strings to pluck, and the fingers to use.

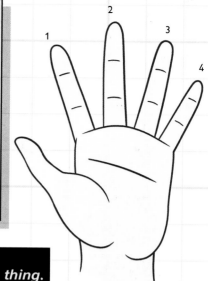

PLAY CHORDS

Before you can play a solo guitar riff, you need to know your chords. Strumming two or more strings together in the right musical combination results in you playing a guitar chord. Learning to play chords is challenging but fun. The easiest three to learn are A, D, and E major as they don't involve complicated hand manoeuvres. Some famous songs use only these three chords, such as the Rolling Stones' *The last time*, Queen's *Crazy little thing called love*, and Eric Clapton's *Crossroads*.

"My guitar is not a thing. It is an extension of myself. It is who I am."

Joan Jett (1958–), American singer and guitarist

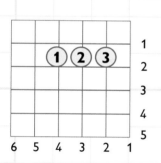

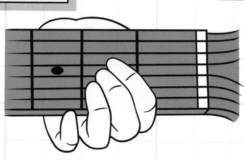

A MAJOR

- Take your plastic pick in hand. You can use your thumb instead, but using a pick is often easier at the start.
- For this chord, strings 1, 5, and 6 are not used.
- Place finger 1 (forefinger) on the second fret of string 4 (D).
- Place finger 2 (middle) on the second fret of string 3 (G).
- Place finger 3 (ring finger) on the second fret of string 2 (B).
- Use your pick to strike strings 2, 3, and 4 to play the A major chord.

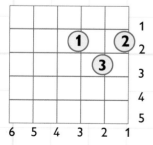

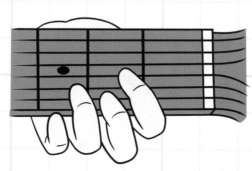

D MAJOR

- For this chord, strings 4, 5, and 6 are not used.
- Place finger 1 (forefinger) on the second fret of string 3 (G).
- Place finger 3 (ring finger) on the third fret of string 2 (B).
- Place finger 2 (middle finger) on the second fret of string 1 (E).
- Use your pick to strike strings 1, 2, and 3 to play the D major chord.

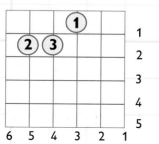

E MAJOR

- For this chord, strings 1, 2, and 6 are not used.
- Place finger 2 (middle) on the second fret of string 5 (A).
- Place finger 3 (ring) on the second fret of string 4 (D).
- Place finger 1 (forefinger) on the first fret of string 3 (G).
- Use your pick to strike strings 3, 4, and 5 to play the E major chord.

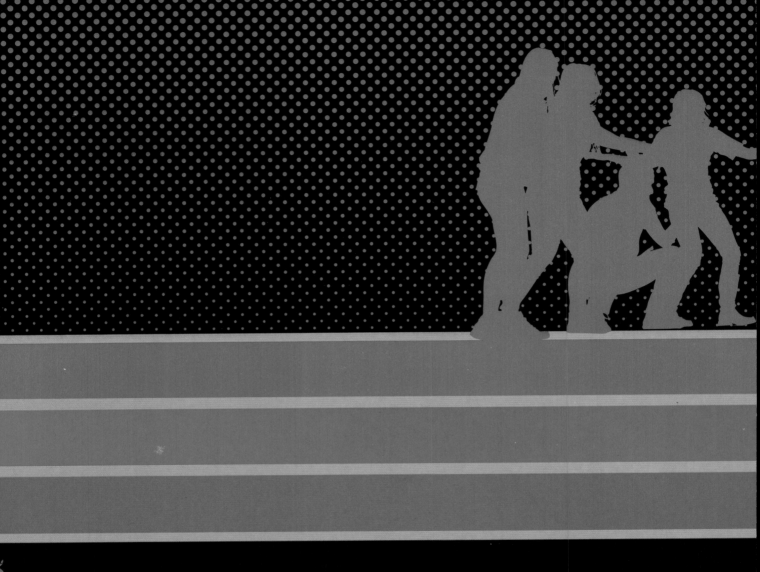

DaNCe

In the earliest communities, dance was essential
to survival. Tribes used dance to learn how to
work and hunt together. Today, dancing is more
of a pleasurable pursuit, and anything goes in the
modern world. Be it budding ballerina or break-dancer,
solo star or group effort, routines set to music or
simply silence, there are lots of opportunities to
make your move. Just put your best foot forward.

STEP BACK IN TIME

As long as there have been people, there has been dance. Over time, different dances have developed across countries and cultures, and the main types of dance are now internationally recognized. Today, the power of television ensures the best performers are seen by the eyes of the world, turning them into global superstars.

c. 60,000–40,000 BCE: Aboriginal people settle in Australia. It is now widely believed that they communicated their stories through dance.

c. 10,000 BCE: Rock art discovered in southern Africa depicts prehistoric dancers. These pictures are made by the San people, who are hunter-gatherers. San shamans perform trance-like dances to capture energy from the spirit world.

c. 4,000 BCE: In many ancient civilizations, dancing before the gods is a temple ritual. Egyptian priests and priestesses play harps and pipes, and perform ritual dances.

c. 1100–221 BCE: In Ancient China, the classic *Book of Songs* chronicles celebratory dance festivals during the Zhou dynasty. Many of the dances in Ancient China are based around farming duties.

c. 700 BCE: The games at Olympia, Ancient Greece, open with performances by the temple dancers. The choros, a dance for the gods, later becomes a part of Greek theatre.

c. 100 CE: In India's Hindu temples, priestesses perform dances involving formal hand movements. Bharata natyam is a similar dance still performed today.

c. 14th century: Written steps from European country dances are described in the manuscript *Le Livre Des Basse-Danses*. This is one of the earliest existing examples of dance steps.

15th century: German guilds of tradespeople have their own group dances. These are performed on special days during the year, and participants are very competitive.

1581: Ballet becomes known in France. At a wedding, the director of court festivals creates *Ballet Comique de la Reine*, the first dramatic ballet.

16th century: Many African peoples are enslaved in America at this time. To lift their spirits and keep their old traditions alive, these African peoples often dance together, ensuring the connection to their continent is not lost.

1661: Dance enthusiast King Louis XIV forms the Académie Royale de Danse in Paris, and later creates the Académie Royale de Musique. They merge to form the Paris Opera, still in existence today.

1681: It's a female first when Pierre Beauchamp and Jean-Baptiste Lully write *Le Triomphe de l'Amour*, which stars Mlle de LaFontaine (1655–1738), the first woman to dance professionally in a ballet.

c. 1700s: In Ireland, dance masters travel from village to village, teaching people different dance routines. Dances are performed with lots of foot percussion, called "battering".

1700s: Ballet spreads across Europe, becoming a large spectacle attended by many people.

1723: Brazil's popular carnival in Rio de Janeiro begins as a celebration before Lent. The most famous dance is the samba. The carnival is still known for its colourful dancing and music today.

1760: A dance called the quadrille becomes well known. This lively routine begins with two couples and finishes with four couples positioned on each side of an imaginary square. Modern square dancing developed from the quadrille.

1780s: First becoming fashionable in Vienna, Austria, the waltz spreads to dance floors in other countries around Europe. Even as late as 1825, the waltz was considered indecent in the UK!

1828: Controversial minstrel dancing gets under way at comic variety shows, led by white performer Thomas Dartmouth "Daddy" Rice (1808–60) who appears in black make-up as a character called Jim Crow. The shows are packed with singing and dancing.

1830–50: During the Romantic period of ballet, female dancers gain recognition by developing their technical and artistic abilities. Until this point, male dancers were the stars of the stage.

1868: Bring on the burlesque! British dancer Lydia Thompson (1838–1908) and her British Blondes take burlesque dancing to the USA. The show's saucy singing, dancing, and comedy makes Thompson a household name.

1890: A rebellion against traditional ballet begins. This period marks the birth of modern dance, in which strong-minded independent dancers and choreographers want to break away from earlier styles of dance and create new moves and techniques.

1890s: Public dance halls are constructed, specifically for the pursuit of dancing. Ordinary people had missed out on aristocratic balls, but now they can experience social dancing for themselves.

1892: The world's most famous ballet premieres in St Petersburg, Russia. *The Nutcracker* is choreographed by Russian dancer Lev Ivanov (1834–1901), with music by the great composer Pyotr Tchaikovsky (1840–93).

1893: A folk dance society is established in Stockholm, Sweden. The Industrial Revolution in Europe makes people nostalgic for the past, so other communities set up their own folk dance societies.

1905: American dancer Isadora Duncan (1877–1927) creates the first school of modern dance in Berlin, Germany.

1906: Aged six years old, twinkletoes himself Fred Astaire (1899–1987) makes his stage debut with sister Adele at a theatre in New Jersey, USA.

1909: The first unofficial world championship of Dancesport is held. This is the internationally recognized style for competitive ballroom and Latin dancing.

1909: The ballet company Ballets Russes de Serge Diaghilev opens in Russia. This marks a move away from Romantic ballet, bringing in an exciting era of modern ballet.

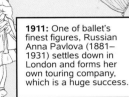

1911: One of ballet's finest figures, Russian Anna Pavlova (1881–1931) settles down in London and forms her own touring company, which is a huge success.

1910s: Married couple Irene and Vernon Castle make ballroom dancing popular in the USA. The foxtrot becomes a favourite of the ballroom dances.

1920s: The Charleston arrives on the dance scene. The steps and kicks are enjoyed by participants. The faster lindy hop is another dance that proves a hit at this time.

1920s: American musicals develop the European folk tradition of the double storey. This involves dancers in one circle standing or sitting on the shoulders of dancers in another circle. This is shown to spectacular effect.

1927: American dancer and choreographer Martha Graham (1894–1991) opens up her school of contemporary dance in New York, USA.

1930: The Camargo Society, founded to promote British dancers and choreographers, showcases its first evening of ballet in London.

1934: Aged 15, English ballerina Margot Fonteyn (1919–91) makes her first appearance, performing as a snowflake in *The Nutcracker*.

1950s: Dancing to rock n' roll music is all the rage. Couples reinvent old steps from the Charleston, with the man taking the lead.

1950s: This decade sees the creation of discotheques (nightclubs in which people dance to popular music), which prove popular with young people.

1958: Dancer and choreographer Alvin Ailey (1931–89) establishes the American Dance Theatre, with the intention of bringing African and American modern dance traditions to the world.

1970s: Glitter balls, ahoy! Helped by *Saturday Night Fever*, disco dancing takes over nightclubs and dance halls, with lasers and light shows adding to the fun.

1989: The English National Ballet evolves from London's Festival Ballet. Today, it is one of the world's leading ballet companies, performing regular global tours.

1964: After Margot Fonteyn (1919–91) and Rudolf Nureyev (1938–93) dance together in *Swan Lake* in Vienna, Austria, they receive 89 curtain calls! They later perform together in *Romeo and Juliet*, *Giselle*, and *Les Sylphides*.

c. 1971: A new dance style, called hip-hop, takes off in New York, USA. Young African Americans enjoy performing this type of dance.

1992: Spanish superstar Joaquín Cortés (1969–) forms his flamenco dance company and goes on to perform around the world.

1994: Based on traditional Irish step dancing, *Riverdance* is first seen during the Eurovision Song Contest.

1995: A controversial version of *Swan Lake* by British dancer and choreographer Matthew Bourne (1960–) breaks with tradition. Instead of delicate female dancers, the swans in the show are played by men in feathery trousers. The modern interpretation stuns audiences, but goes on to become a huge hit.

2004: First screened in the UK, *Strictly Come Dancing* is a dancing competition in which professionals pair up with celebrities to learn and perform dances. The show's format has now been taken up by at least 32 more countries.

2009: Street dance troupe *Diversity* wins *Britain's Got Talent*. A year later, acrobatic dance group *Spelbound* wins the series. In addition, dance competitions are shown on television, inviting members of the public to perform.

LET'S DANCE

All performers use skill, stamina, and flexibility to shine on the dance floor. They usually follow a choreographed series of steps in time to music. The type of music influences the style of the dance and the movements of the dancers. Here's your fast-paced, rhythm-packed guide to the most celebrated steps around. Keep up!

VIENNESE WALTZ
This whirling, swirling ballroom dance became popular in the 1800s. The name waltz comes from the German word meaning "to spin".

BALLROOM
This sophisticated genre includes a variety of dances involving couples who perform a set pattern of steps to melodic music. Though usually performed at social gatherings, more accomplished ballroom dancers participate in competitions.

TANGO
Started as a South American street dance in the mid-19th century, the tango is a passionate and dramatic dance. Tango is also the name for the music that accompanies this style of dance.

FOXTROT
Popular in the 1910s, the graceful foxtrot is made up of long, gliding, smooth steps. American dancing legends Fred Astaire (1899–1987) and Gene Kelly (1912–96) performed perfect foxtrots in their films.

QUICKSTEP
An even faster version of the foxtrot, this ballroom dance was developed in the 1920s, with lots of movement around the dance floor.

JIVE
A hit during the mid-20th century, this energetic style of dance includes a number of different jives, such as the jitterbug, swing, and boogie-woogie.

LATIN
The Latin American culture is brought to life by this mix of spirited and sensual dances. Characterized by fluid hip movements and passionate interaction, couples dance closely together to the infectious, upbeat tempo of the music.

SALSA
Enjoying a 21st-century revival, popular salsa came from Cuba in the 1940s. The four-step beat consists of two quick steps, a slow step, and a pause.

SAMBA
With its roots in Africa and the Caribbean, this lively Brazilian dance is performed at high speed. The dance is performed at Brazil's famous annual carnival.

RUMBA
All about the rhythm, the rumba's basic step is slow-quick-quick, accompanied by plenty of hip action.

FOLK AND GLOBAL

Traditional dances originating among the people of a nation or region fall into this category. Locals usually perform the dances to traditional music played by other members of the community. They learn the steps from watching their elders. Dances are informal and rarely performed on stage.

TRIBAL

African ceremonies often include tribal dances performed to the beat of a drum. Whether at weddings or funerals, locals are united by taking part in the dances.

> **"When the music changes, so does the dance."**
>
> *African proverb*

FLAMENCO

Finding its feet in the villages of Andalucia, Spain, flamenco is both a style of music and dance with a strong rhythm. Dancers dress up to perform in time with the guitar music.

COUNTRY AND WESTERN

Associated with the USA's history of country and western music, couples perform line dances while dressed in typical cowboy clothing. Yee haw!

FREESTYLE

Convention goes out the window when it comes to the freestyle genre of dance. People make up their own moves to music, being as innovative and creative as they want in this relatively new dance phenomenon that breaks with past tradition.

BALLET

This famous form of artistic and theatrical dance uses graceful, flowing movements to tell a story to instrumental music. Dancers keep their bodies in peak condition to perform the intricate steps.

JAZZ

A rhythmic and improvised (made up spontaneously) dance, jazz is influenced by the distinctive sounds of jazz music.

DISCO

Since the 1970s, people have gathered in clubs to dance to popular songs with strong, repetitive beats. Though some dancers follow set steps, many come up with their own moves to light up the dance floor.

TRADITIONAL

Many of the dances in the traditional genre are long established and well known around the world. Though they have taken time to develop, most of them are characterized by set repetitive movements to different styles of music.

TAP

This style is instantly recognizable by the rhythmic tapping of dancers' shoes, which have pieces of metal attached to the soles and heels.

BREAK-DANCE

This form of solo dancing involves rapid acrobatic moves in which different parts of the body touch the ground. It is normally performed to hip-hop music.

DANCE

I'M IN THE MOOD FOR DANCING

You probably know what gets you up and on the dance floor, but what about all the other dancers around the world? Throughout history and across cultures, people have found very different reasons to get moving. Whether for tradition, ritual, celebration, hope, fear, competition, or fitness, the motivations change, but the desire to dance remains.

HERE'S HOPING

Culture and dance are closely linked for native tribes. Dance is a way to celebrate nature, to demonstrate prayer, and to worship the gods. The Native Americans of the Great Plains would dance for their gods, expressing frustration at the poverty and despair they faced. This 1912 illustration of a Native American ghost dance captures the mood. Usually performed to a drumbeat, dancing was a focus for their feelings and an expression of hope for the future.

TYING THE KNOT

In many African cultures, it is traditional to perform dances at celebrations, such as marriages. This creates a positive atmosphere and brings good fortune for the couple's commitment. For King Letsie III of Lesotho's wedding in 2000, locals performed a special warriors' battle dance in the village (shown here). Young women in the Venda tribe of South Africa get ready for marriage by dancing the domba. They form a close chain for the routine, which requires timing and teamwork.

WAGING WAR

Combat has long been a reason for dancing, to strengthen warriors' hands for fighting and to bring about unity before battle commences. As well as preparing for combat, war dances can also be a celebration of victory afterwards. New Zealand's Maori people performed the traditional haka dance before and after battle. The country's national rugby team now perform the haka before kick-off to mentally prepare for the game.

> *"Dancing is the loftiest, the most moving, the most beautiful of the arts, because it is no mere translation or abstraction from life; it is life itself."*
>
> Havelock Ellis (1859–1939), British writer and psychologist

TOP OF THE CROPS

The production of a bountiful harvest at the end of a bumper farming year is marked around the world by festival dances. As well as celebrating the feast to come, the ritual is believed to prepare the earth for next year's harvest. In India, the harvest festival dance is called the wangala. Here, the dancers of the Koya tribe in Orissa play drums and wear headdresses of cattle horns, shells, and feathers.

IT'S A CELEBRATION

Special events in a person's life, such as coming of age, the start of a school year, or even the end of a life, are cause for a celebratory dance in some cultures. The Tujia people of China use a funeral dance called the sayi'erhe to show their prayers for a happy ending to a person's life. On a less serious note, some Japanese communities pound steamed rice during their coming-of-age dance. Sounds like any excuse for a party!

RAINMAKERS

Some cultures believe that it is possible to influence the weather using the power of dance. Rain is essential to ensure a good harvest, so many farming communities perform ritual dances to bring on the showers. As far back as Ancient Egypt, people have regarded rain as a good omen. Indian Hopi priests often wear feathers and the colour turquoise to represent the wind and rain they are wishing for in their dances.

KEEP FIT

In the past, sailors would perform a dance called the hornpipe to ensure they got some exercise while on board ships at sea. Experts agree that dancing is one of the best ways to keep fit. That is why so many gyms now offer dance classes as an alternative to traditional weights and exercise machines. Energetic routines can burn as many calories as fast walking and downhill skiing, and for dancing divas, this is often a preferable option to give your body a full workout. You can do it anywhere and it costs nothing, so turn on some tunes and get moving!

CALL OF NATURE

Studies of New Guinea's birds of paradise have found they like to shake a tail feather as much as the rest of us. They perform dances in the forest, displaying their dazzlingly bright plumage to potential mates. These courtship dances have been compared to people dancing at a disco in the hope of attracting a partner.

HEALTHY COMPETITION

Competitive spirit goes hand in hand with professional dancing. During the 1920s and 1930s, competitions were held to see how long people could keep dancing, which ended up lasting weeks at a time! Today, it's more about performance excellence. Judges look for technical ability and artistic expression in the dancers.

HOW TO:

LET'S GET PHYSICAL

WARM UP

Dancing can put a huge strain on the body, as the joints and muscles are moved into all kinds of different positions that they do not usually adopt. If you don't warm up, you run the risk of injury, and that's no fun at all. Imagine being at the disco watching your mates bust some moves, while you're sitting on the sidelines. Once you make stretching and warming-up exercises part of your normal dancing routine, you'll go through the motions without even thinking about it. Preparing your body by loosening the key joints and muscles gets you in the groove for dancing, but it also gets your brain active as well. As the warm-up exercises make your body ready, your mind also becomes sharper from the movement and more focused on the dance routines to come. Wear lots of layers to start and take them off as you get warmer.

> *"Dance... even if you have nowhere to do it but in your own living room."*
>
> Baz Luhrmann (1962–),
> Australian film director, from the song
> Everybody's free (to wear sunscreen)

Walk or jog with your arms aloft to warm up your body in preparation for dance activity.

THE HEAT IS ON

Slowly start the warm-up exercises. The first thing to do is raise your body temperature, and you can try this in different ways. If space is limited, walk briskly around the room with your arms above your head. Repeat this until you can feel yourself getting warmer. Alternatively, try jogging on the spot for a few minutes until you feel your heart rate speeding up and your skin heating up. Exercises like these ensure blood is flowing freely to your muscles and your joints are well lubricated. As your heart rate picks up, more oxygen travels to the muscles, getting them ready for movement.

If all this talk of dancing is inspiring you, hold your horses! You can't get dancing right away. Warming up is very important before you start practising a new dance routine. It keeps you supple and also ensures you don't pull a muscle. Some basic warm-up exercises will get your body in tip-top condition for dancing. Then, once you've danced your cares away, it's time to cool off.

Bend your neck up and down. Repeat this five times.

Rotate your wrist to loosen it. Do both wrists five times.

STRETCH YOURSELF

To make sure you don't miss out any part of your body, start the stretching with your head and work your way down to your feet. Make your stretches slow and relaxed, and take calm, deep breaths throughout.

- Stand still and slowly move your head from side to side. Repeat five times.
- Slowly rotate your head five times.
- Rotate each shoulder five times.
- Bend and straighten both elbows five times.
- Point and flex your fingers on both hands five times.
- Rotate your hips five times.
- Bend and straighten your knees five times.
- Rotate each ankle five times.
- Point and flex your toes on both feet five times.

Warning! It is easy for beginners to overextend when doing a lunge stretch and even pull a hamstring. So, take care and only stretch as far as feels comfortable.

LUNGE STRETCH

A lunge stretch is a good way to stretch your legs, particularly the quad muscles and hamstrings.
- Push one of your legs forward, with your back leg left straight. The front leg should be bent at approximately 90 degrees, with your knee directly above your foot. Check that your hips are facing your leading leg.
- Place your hands flat on the floor, either side of your leading leg.
- Move backwards gently, feeling the back leg lengthening.
- Gently push the stomach towards the knee.
- Hold the stretch for ten seconds and repeat three times for each leg.

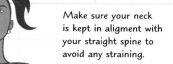

Make sure your neck is kept in aligment with your straight spine to avoid any straining.

THIGH STRETCH

Stretching the delicate inner thigh area of the body helps to protect it from any injuries caused by dancing.
- Sit on the floor with your knees bent.
- Bring your feet together and let your legs fall to either side.
- Ensure your spine is straight and press your knees towards the floor with your elbows.
- Move your stomach forward towards your feet, keeping your back straight at all times.
- Breathe in and out deeply five times while in this position, and move your upper body closer to the floor every time you breathe out.

BUILD A ROUTINE

You're warm, you're stretched. Now it is time to plan a dance-based start-up routine. You can incorporate different moves from fitness workouts you've seen, as well as some of your favourite moves. Try star jumps, combat punches, and low kicks to start. If the low kicks are going well, you can build up to higher kicks. Keep your moves simple and repetitive. The whole routine should be no more than five moves repeated in the same order. This allows you to concentrate on perfecting your steps without getting lost trying to remember the order of too many complicated moves.

Include star jumps, in which you jump while spreading your arms and legs at the same time.

Include jogging on the spot while doing punches in a combat style.

Include kicks, in which you push out with your alternate legs as far back or up as is comfortable.

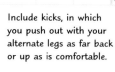

TOP TIPS

- Put your favourite upbeat music on for the warm-up and cool-off periods, as this will make you enjoy the exercises more.
- Always leave enough time for your warm up and cool off. Never think to skip them or you'll run the risk of injury.
- Drink plenty of water before you dance and while you're dancing to keep hydrated.

Slow movements and gentle stretching will wind your body down.

COOL OFF

Once you've danced your neon leg warmers off, don't forget to give your body a chance to cool down. Some slow, relaxing exercises will take your body back to its normal resting state. Try leaning your hands against a wall while slowly pushing each leg forwards and backwards, or sit on the floor, stretch your arms out, and gently push them towards the floor. This avoids any aches and pains in the morning! As you cool down, put your layers of clothing back on to keep warm.

NEVER-ENDING STORY

When fabulous footwork and tantalizing tales combine, the result is a musical. Theatres are packed with audiences who delight in this mix of dance and drama. Some of the greatest musicals showcase a specific style of dance within the story, which captures the public imagination. If you're sitting comfortably, we'll begin.

42ND STREET

The musical *42nd Street* tapped into a popular style of dance. Based on the novel of the same name by Bradford Ropes, the story describes a director's attempt to stage a successful musical during the Great Depression. When American choreographer Gower Champion started his stage adaptation with 40 pairs of feet tap-dancing as the curtain came up, a hit show was born. Audiences loved the musical's contrasting displays of spectacular tap-dancing against the grey backdrop of economic depression.

THE NUTCRACKER

The most popular ballet of all time, *The Nutcracker* is a choreographed version of *The Nutcracker and the Mouse King* by E T A Hoffman. This is the story of a German girl who is given a nutcracker in the shape of a man as a gift. After the nutcracker battles with toy soldiers and a mouse king, it turns into a prince and takes the girl to magic lands, before she wakes to find it was all a dream. In 1892, *The Nutcracker* was made into a ballet by Russian dancers Marius Petipa and Led Ivanov. It was recreated in 2002 with visual twists by British ballet choreographer Matthew Bourne.

> *"Life will go on as long as there is someone to sing, to dance, to tell stories, and to listen."*
>
> Oren Lyons (1930–),
> Native American speaker
> and campaigner

A CHORUS LINE

The step kick became an iconic dance move after its inclusion in *A Chorus Line*. Based on the 1976 book by American authors James Kirkwood and Nicholas Dante, the musical told the tale of Broadway dancers in America auditioning to be part of a chorus line. The characters lift their legs up high and kick out as they try to impress their audience. Today, *A Chorus Line* remains the longest-running Broadway musical originally produced in the USA.

OKLAHOMA!

Barn dancing was the main attraction in *Oklahoma!*, the first musical by America's successful songwriting partnership Rogers and Hammerstein. The musical is based on Lynn Riggs' 1931 play *Green Grow the Lilacs*, which tells the story of a romance between a cowboy and a farm girl. American director Susan Stroman gave *Oklahoma!* an award-winning treatment in 1999, which included a fun-filled barn dance to the song *The farmer and the cowman*.

GREASE

Born to hand jive, baby went the song, and the cast of the popular American musical demonstrated the hand jive to spectacular effect. Set in a high school in 1959, *Grease* follows a group of teenagers through the highs and lows of friendship and love. Hot on the heels of the 1978 hit film *Grease*, starring John Travolta and Olivia Newton-John, the musical brought the sounds and moves of early rock n' roll to the stage.

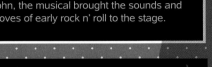

CATS

What would poet T S Eliot (1888–1965) have thought if he'd known his 1939 poetry collection *Old Possum's Book of Practical Cats* was going to be turned into a musical? In 1981, Andrew Lloyd Webber's award-wining interpretation used dancers dressed up as cat characters, including Grizabella, Old Deuteronomy, and Mister Mistoffelees, who adopted exaggerated feline mannerisms in their routines. This catapulted the show to huge success around the world, becoming one of the longest-running musicals in Broadway history.

CHICAGO

A spoof on the idea that the press portrays criminals as stars, the musical *Chicago* was based on a 1926 play of the same name about true crimes. What set it apart from the rest was the use of Fosse choreography. This unusual style was devised by American dancer Robert "Bob" Fosse (1927–87), who chose to focus on different parts of dancers' bodies to make new moves. The stomach and shoulders were emphasized instead of the traditional legs and feet. A musical called *Fosse* about the dancer's great contribution to choreography opened on Broadway in 1999, and his influence is still seen on stage today.

WEST SIDE STORY

In 1957, this famous American musical about rival street gangs in New York caused a sensation. Based on William Shakespeare's 16th-century play about star-crossed lovers, *Romeo and Juliet*, *West Side Story* gave the tragic tale a modern update. When Tony of the Jets falls in love with Maria of the Sharks, there is no happy ending for the doomed lovers. American choreographer Jerome Robbins came up trumps when he introduced a new style of theatrical dance mixed with traditional ballet to represent the old and new influences on this classic love story.

GET ON YOUR FEET

If you've ever watched a dancer perform and dreamed of being in their shoes, choosing the correct footwear is the first step. The style of shoe depends on the type of dance you're taking up, but whether you're going glam or on a shoestring budget, options are available to suit everyone. As long as your shoes are comfortable and practical, your posture and movements will feel right and you won't put a foot wrong.

BALLET SHOES

Classic ballet shoes allow the dancer to stand *en pointe* (on tiptoe). The satin exterior makes the shoes appear soft, but they are actually stiff due to a hard layer of hessian and paper in the design. Don't expect your ballet shoes to last a long time. They fray and wear out very quickly. Dancers in leading ballet companies get through at least ten pairs a month!

DISCO BOOTS

If you're going dancing, give yourself a lift with some classic platform boots. These elevated soles made of cork, wood, plastic, or rubber are a throwback to the disco days of the 1970s when this style of music ruled the dance floor. Look out for loud colours, garish patterns, and skyscraper heels to ensure you steal the limelight. A word of advice – if you're a beginner at disco dancing, start with a lower heel to avoid breaking your ankle!

PAINTED FEET

Some styles of dance put the feet first. For example, in the classical Indian dance of bharata natyam, performers don't even wear shoes. Instead, they decorate their feet with henna (a flowering plant used to dye the skin). The colourful patterns of the feet are designed to match their painted hands. The dancers also don ankle bells to make themselves heard as they move.

TOP TIPS

- Be practical. Don't choose a shoe just because you like the look of it. Go for one that will work best for you with your new style of dance.
- Choose a snug, but not tight, fit.
- Make sure you try the shoes before you buy. Experienced salespeople will spend time helping you to find the proper fit and style for you.
- Don't don your dancing shoes 24/7 as they will wear out quickly.

TAP SHOES

Everyone will hear you coming if you take up tap-dancing! When this style of dance emerged in the early 20th century, tap shoes had coins or nails hammered into the toes and heels to make the loud tapping sound. Today, metal taps are the norm, and many have adjustable screws so dancers can make a variety of sounds. Leather-soled shoes are the best bet for beginners as rubber-soled versions can stick.

STILTS

You'll need to perform your best balancing act for this one! In parts of southern and western Africa, dancers do their routines on stilts up to 2 m (6 ft) in height. The risk of danger is all part of the fun, and if you find your balance, it is said to symbolize the wisdom of humankind. Stilt dancers feature in festivals around the world, such as La Rioja in Spain, Deventer in the Netherlands, and Namur in Belgium.

TRAINERS

Many people live in their trainers already, but freestyle and street dancers may wear them for comfort during their routines. As dancers must be able to jump, turn, and point with ease, a good pair of trainers can be just the job. Experts try and test specialized versions of dance trainers, designed with these moves in mind.

"Dancing is the poetry of the foot."

John Dryden (1631–1700), English poet and dramatist

BALLROOM SHOES

If you're going for a twirl, choose your ballroom dancing shoes with care. For men, these shoes are usually black lace ups with a flat heel for the ballroom dances, going up to a small heel for the Latin routines. There is more variety for women, depending on the dance. Most designs are open- or closed-toe sandals. Heels are slim or flared. Slim heels are ideal for making moves such as turns, while flared heels suit the Latin dances, which require more stability on the floor.

I BET YOU LOOK GOOD ON THE DANCE FLOOR

Every so often, history reveals a shining star of the dance floor. Some dancers are blessed with innate ability, while others devote their lives to practice that pays off. These legends will never be forgotten because their names are forever linked to the style of dance they performed. Take a turn around the floor with these famous faces, but let them lead!

ANNA PAVLOVA

Russian ballerina Anna Pavlova (1881–1931) once said that she wanted to "dance for everybody in the world!" and she was almost as good as her word. Between 1910 and 1925, she performed nearly 4,000 times across Europe, the Americas, Asia, and Africa. Known for how well she could take a story and translate it into dance, Pavlova was an international inspiration.

VASLAV NIJINSKY

Noted for the spring in his step, Russian dancer Vaslav Nijinsky (1890–1950) made a leap of faith in *Le spectre de la rose* when he famously jumped from a window into the night sky. He is best remembered for his portrayal of a faun in the controversial ballet *L'après-midi d'un faune* (above). On the opening night, audience members declared the ballet obscene.

MARTHA GRAHAM

Pioneering the importance of breathing techniques in performance, American dancer Martha Graham (1894–1991) based her findings on the principles of "contraction and release". She used this to found an innovative style of modern dance. Her name lives on in the world's oldest modern dance company, the Martha Graham Dance Company, set up in 1926.

FRED ASTAIRE & GINGER ROGERS

For many, Fred Astaire (1899–1987) was the greatest dancer of all as he swept across stages and screens around the world. In 1933, Astaire and fellow American Ginger Rogers (1911–95) danced together for the first time on film in *Flying down to Rio*. It was the beginning of a beautiful partnership. Sharing the screen for nine films in total, the two remain ballroom dancing's most famous couple.

FRANKIE MANNING

New York's Savoy Ballroom swung to life during the 1930s thanks to the energizing efforts of American dancer and choreographer Frankie Manning (1914–2009). A master of the lindy hop dance, he introduced the lindy air step and the synchronized lindy routine for group performances. As a result of these exciting additions, the classic Charleston-based lindy hop was revived, making its move from ballrooms to theatres and televisions.

PATRICK SWAYZE

Heart-throb American actor and dancer Patrick Swayze (1952–2009) hit the big time when he played dance instructor Johnny Castle in the 1987 blockbuster *Dirty Dancing*. The story of young love at a 1960s holiday camp was a favourite with teenage audiences. Swayze's super-smooth moves and the famous lift-in-the-lake scene turned him into a star.

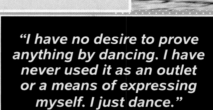

SAMMY DAVIS JNR.

As one of America's first black stars, tap-dancing legend Sammy Davis Junior (1925–90) was loved for his dazzling performances in Las Vegas and on Broadway, New York. Tap-dancing was not his only talent. Hailed as "the world's greatest entertainer", the charismatic all-rounder also sang, acted, and performed comedy routines.

> *"I have no desire to prove anything by dancing. I have never used it as an outlet or a means of expressing myself. I just dance."*
>
> Fred Astaire (1899–1987),
> American ballroom dancer

JOHN TRAVOLTA

Though skilled at singing and acting, the main string in John Travolta's bow is disco dancing. Blowing audiences away with his coordinated and complex routines in 1970s films such as *Saturday Night Fever* and *Grease*, Travolta became an overnight sensation. Young people copied his iconic moves, with the point-and-shake step still instantly recognizable today.

MICHAEL FLATLEY

The undisputed Lord of the Dance, Irish-American Michael Flatley (1958–) found fame in dance shows, including *Riverdance*, *Feet of Flames*, and *Celtic Tiger*. Flatley's footprint is now embedded in dance history, after he broke tap-dancing records in 1998 (35 taps per second!), and became the world's highest-paid dancer in both 1999 and 2000.

MICHAEL JACKSON

King of Pop Michael Jackson (1958–2009) started out as a child star in the group *The Jackson Five* alongside his brothers. A spectacular solo career followed, involving multiple albums and groundbreaking dance routines. He is the first and only dancer in the genre of pop music to be included in the Dance Hall of Fame.

DARCEY BUSSELL

Widely regarded as one of the greatest ballerinas of all time, English dancer Darcy Bussell (1969–) was a Principal Dancer at the Royal Ballet in London for 17 years. Now retired, Bussell has received awards and accolades for her beautiful performances and, in 2009, she became a judge on television's popular show *Strictly Come Dancing*.

DIVERSITY

British dance troupe *Diversity* is leading the way for modern street dance. Best known for pipping suprise singing sensation Susan Boyle to the post in the *Britain's Got Talent* final of 2009, Diversity is made up of choreographer Ashley Banjo (1988–) and ten more members. The award-winning troupe create visually stunning routines to their own interpretations of famous songs.

HOW TO:

PERFORM
THE CLASSIC
CHARLESTON

PERFORM A
DISCO DANCE
ROUTINE

STEPPIN' OUT

Mastering the moves of a famous dance is great fun. It's good to start with an easy routine that can provide the basis for learning more complicated dances. Try a blast from the past with a classic Charleston. The simple steps are repetitive, yet energetic and exciting. If you want a go at something more modern, turn disco dancer with funky footsteps from the 1970s. Groovy, baby!

52

CLASSIC CHARLESTON

When the Charleston dance took over the floor during the 1920s, people assumed it must have been only for professionals. The flappers (as they were known) soon had it down to a fine art. As the first social dance that didn't require a partner, the Charleston steps are ideal for you to try on your own.

1. Step forward on your left foot.

Though full of character, the Charleston's simple arm and leg movements ensure the dance is easy for beginners to learn.

2. Trying to keep your knees together, bring your right foot around and touch the floor with it in front of your left foot.

> **"I don't want people who want to dance; I want people who have to dance."**
>
> *George Balanchine (1904–83), Russian ballet choreographer*

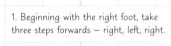

1. Beginning with the right foot, take three steps forwards — right, left, right.

2. Hit the left foot against the right foot and clap your hands. This move is known as the hustle.

Disco dances are typically composed of several simple steps, making them a great place for disco divas to get started.

7. Step forwards and backwards, tilting your shoulders up and down.

8. Work your hands and shake your hips in time to the music.

DISCO DANCE ROUTINE

The 1977 film *Saturday Night Fever* took dance floors by storm. Choreographed dance steps were played out to the beat of disco music, spun by DJs. Disco touches on elements of Latin dance, such as hip and pelvic movements, and plenty of turns.

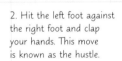

3. Bring your right foot back around to where it started and put your weight on it.

4. Trying to keep your knees together, bring your left foot around and touch the floor with it behind your right foot. Repeat steps 1–4.

5. Repeat, but this time kick your right leg up when you go forward on step 2.

6. Put your left foot back on the ground as far as it will go when you go backwards on step 4.

7. Now get your arms in on the action. Swing your arms forward opposite of your feet, as you would naturally if you were walking, but swing high. Once the arm moves are paired with the kick step, you are dancing the Charleston. Go, flapper!

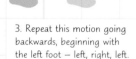

3. Repeat this motion going backwards, beginning with the left foot — left, right, left.

4. Hit the right foot against the left foot and clap your hands. Do the hustle!

5. This first forward movement can be repeated from side to side — three steps to the right, then clap, then three steps to the left, then clap.

6. Step from side to side and turn full circle after each step.

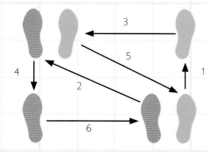

9. Step forward on your right foot (1). Put your left foot diagonally forward to the left (2), so it is level with the right foot. Bring your right foot in next to your left foot (3). Then repeat backwards, starting on the left foot. Step backwards on your left foot (4). Put your right foot diagonally backwards to the right (5). Bring your left foot in next to your right foot (6). This move is called the box step.

10. John Travolta had better watch out for you! Move your left arm diagonally across your body and point your forefinger downwards.

11. Then, in one quick movement, move your left arm back and up, pointing your forefinger to the sky on the diagonal. You're performing the point!

12. Between moves, keep stepping from side to side, pushing your hips out. This is a typical filler activity between disco moves, but it looks very effective.

DANCING IN THE STREET

Who needs a dance floor in this day and age? Conventional ballrooms, stages, and studios are a thing of the past for many of today's dancers. Whether taking to the streets or making waves in water, performers continue to find new ways and places to showcase their skills. Maybe one day, we'll be dancing on the ceiling, as Lionel Richie hoped!

IN WATER

At the turn of the 20th century, synchronized swimming – a blend of swimming, dance, and gymnastics – was called water ballet. These movements in water require all the essentials of traditional dance, including timing, strength, grace, and flexibility, not to mention the ability to hold your breath upside down underwater! Aquatic shows around the world push the boat out with amazing colour fountains, lasers, and water cannons to ensure the routines make a splash.

STREET DANCE

Combining hip-hop, robotics, and break-dance in innovative new ways, street dance can literally be performed anywhere. Though the most well-known troupes are hired to perform on stage or in studios, street dance is informal enough for performers to give impromptu displays in public. This was how it all began in New York City during the 1970s. Word has spread, and now street dance is at the very forefront of modern dance, with the characteristically cutting-edge moves appealing to young people in particular.

54

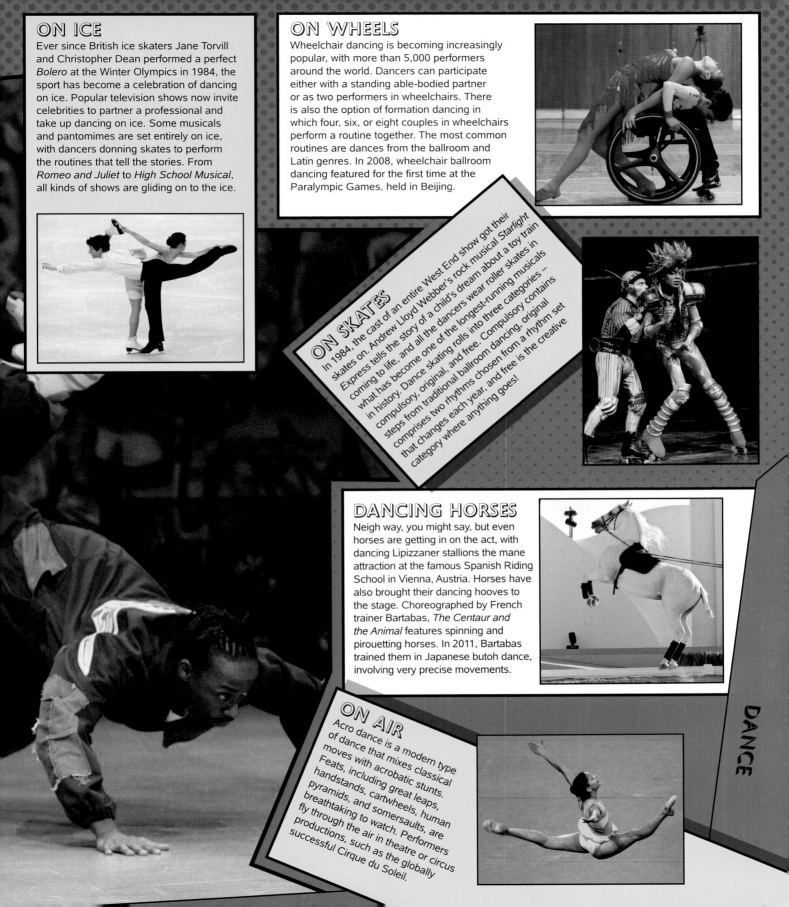

ON ICE

Ever since British ice skaters Jane Torvill and Christopher Dean performed a perfect *Bolero* at the Winter Olympics in 1984, the sport has become a celebration of dancing on ice. Popular television shows now invite celebrities to partner a professional and take up dancing on ice. Some musicals and pantomimes are set entirely on ice, with dancers donning skates to perform the routines that tell the stories. From *Romeo and Juliet* to *High School Musical*, all kinds of shows are gliding on to the ice.

ON WHEELS

Wheelchair dancing is becoming increasingly popular, with more than 5,000 performers around the world. Dancers can participate either with a standing able-bodied partner or as two performers in wheelchairs. There is also the option of formation dancing in which four, six, or eight couples in wheelchairs perform a routine together. The most common routines are dances from the ballroom and Latin genres. In 2008, wheelchair ballroom dancing featured for the first time at the Paralympic Games, held in Beijing.

ON SKATES

In 1984, the cast of an entire West End show got their skates on. Andrew Lloyd Webber's rock musical *Starlight Express* tells the story of a child's dream about a toy train coming to life, and all the dancers wear roller skates in what has become one of the longest-running musicals in history. Dance skating rolls into three categories — compulsory, original, and free. Compulsory contains steps from traditional ballroom dancing, original comprises two rhythms chosen from a rhythm set that changes each year, and free is the creative category where anything goes!

DANCING HORSES

Neigh way, you might say, but even horses are getting in on the act, with dancing Lipizzaner stallions the mane attraction at the famous Spanish Riding School in Vienna, Austria. Horses have also brought their dancing hooves to the stage. Choreographed by French trainer Bartabas, *The Centaur and the Animal* features spinning and pirouetting horses. In 2011, Bartabas trained them in Japanese butoh dance, involving very precise movements.

ON AIR

Acro dance is a modern type of dance that mixes classical moves with acrobatic stunts. Feats, including great leaps, handstands, cartwheels, human pyramids, and somersaults, are breathtaking to watch. Performers fly through the air in theatre or circus productions, such as the globally successful Cirque du Soleil.

DANCE

MOVERS AND SHAKERS

Hmmm... this lot probably don't look like any dance partners you've ever known, but don't let that put you off. Around the world, performers participate in some very unusual dance routines as part of their cultures. These are often very demanding, requiring even more skill and focus than the mainstream moves with which you are more familiar. Step this way...

LIMBO DANCING

Limbering up is essential for the limbo, in which the dancer bends over backwards to pass under a horizontal pole without knocking it off. The pole is repeatedly lowered after each successful clearance to make it even more difficult. Originating in West Africa, limbo performers today show off their impressive skills at carnivals and celebrations. The dancers may make it look easy, but they are actually incredibly flexible and supple. Don't try this at home!

NOH DANCING

Japanese performers participate in an intricate, powerful form of dance drama called Noh. It is based on the tricky concept of *jo-ha-kyu*, which looks at how all actions should begin slowly, speed up, and then end very quickly. Gesture and breathing are all-important to the dance, which is performed to music. Noh can be slow or fast, short or long. Performers are easy to recognize by their shiny masks and ornate kimonos, as well as their use of props to symbolize the dance themes.

MORRIS DANCING

Starting as a spectacle at local festivals in northern and central parts of England, morris dancing is now displayed all over the world. It used to be performed only by men as part of a ceremonial dance, but today, both sexes participate, often in competitions. Dancers dress alike with team colours, straw hats, white shirts, braces called baldrics, and bells on their socks that ring in time to the music. They hold sticks or handkerchiefs to wave aloft in the group dance.

"The trained dancer must not only have grace and elegance, but also the leap of an Olympic hurdler, the balance of a tightrope walker, and panther-like strength and agility."

Camilla Jessel, author

56

HIGHLAND FLING

This energetic dance of the Scottish Highlands should come with a safety warning! Traditionally, male participants would leap over a targe (shield) with a scary steel spike coming from it. The fear of falling on it certainly encouraged them to jump sky high! Today, the Highland fling is a favourite at global dance competitions. Sporting traditional tartan kilts to represent their Scottish clans, dancers keep their upper bodies taut, letting their legs do all the hard work.

KATHAKALI

You can't miss the kathakali performers! Their layers of eye-catching dramatic make-up, which can take four hours to perfect, are set off by huge kiritams (headdresses) made of wood and studded with glittering gems. Costumes are just as elaborate, with gold and silver details adorning the bright material. This 17th-century Indian dance drama has developed over the years. As well as rhythmic movements of the hands, legs, and body, today's dancers train their facial muscles to express a wide range of emotions for their audience.

WHIRLING DERVISH

Guaranteed to get you in a spin, whirling dervishes are specially trained dancers able to spin around on the spot faster and faster for long periods of time. Originally from Turkey, these Muslim performers appear to go into a trance and believe that they are coming closer to God in this moment. When they come to a stop, they stand perfectly still without giving the slightest impression of dizziness. It's not easy – give it a whirl yourself and see how dizzy you are after only a couple of spins!

COSSACK JUMPER

Groups of usually male Russian soldiers, called Cossacks, look like soldiers going into battle as they dance with swords and long sticks. They literally jump at the chance of a dance competition. Leaps and kicks are regarded as proof of their strength and agility. The higher they go, the higher they are regarded in society. They also have to squat a lot, which requires supreme stamina.

FLASHDANCE

Fun, fleeting fads can fill up discos and dance halls around the world as participants try out the latest new moves. Novelty hit songs or groundbreaking music videos often lead to the creation of a recognized routine of steps that brings people together. Some dances prove so popular that they survive the test of time by making a comeback years later.

> *"It's just a jump to the left,
> And then a step to the right.
> Put your hands on your hips,
> You bring your knees in tight.
> But it's the pelvic thrust
> that really drives you insane,
> Let's do the time warp again."*
>
> Lyrics of The time warp, *taken from*
> *The Rocky Horror Picture Show (1973)*

OOPS UPSIDE YOUR HEAD

Ideal for any lazybones in the crowd, this dance sees participants sitting on the floor in a line, moving their upper bodies and arms from side to side, while alternately touching their hands on the floor. Performed to the tune of The Gap Band's 1979 smash *Oops upside your head*, this dance craze remains very popular, though no one is sure of exactly where it came from.

THE TIME WARP

Featured in the 1973 rock n' roll musical *The Rocky Horror Picture Show* and the film adaptation that followed two years later, *The time warp* is a masterclass in audience participation. The steps of the dance are explained in the lyrics of the song, and the show sees the crowd in costume like the characters and on their feet joining in with all the moves. The simple steps and catchy chorus also make it a party favourite. Altogether now, *It's astounding, time is fleeting…*

CAKEWALK

The cakewalk craze of the 1890s kept everybody sweet. This dance began on sugar-cane plantations where owners would hold dance competitions for African workers. Those with a sweet tooth were keen to get their just desserts – the best movers were given cakes as a prize! Breaking with the traditions of ballroom dancing at that time, the cakewalk was made up of high, strutting steps in a square formation that kept the participants entertained. Don't be shy, give it a try – start strutting!

CONGA

Even if you've got two left feet, there is no excuse not to join the conga. Forming a long line around the room, dancers put their hands on the waist of the person in front and follow the simplest of steps – one, two, three, and kick in time to the beat. This Afro-Cuban dance has found many fans, especially in Miami, USA, where almost 120,000 people formed history's longest conga line in 1988. *Do do do. Come on and do the conga!*

VOGUE

Though many people heard of *Vogue* only when Queen of Pop Madonna released her hit song and music video in 1990, this dramatic dance was actually devised by African- and Latin-American movers living in New York during the 1960s. It's not one for shrinking violets, though, as it involves lots of posing and pouting like a model, accompanied by swift and sharp body movements. Get into diva mode, then *strike a pose, there's nothing to it.*

CHICKEN DANCE

Don't be a chicken! Just puff up your feathers and do your best birdie impression, then you won't go far wrong. Hatched from a novelty song by Swiss accordian player Werner Thomas in the 1950s, *The chicken dance* developed into a tribute to our feathered friends. The steps include making a beak with your hands, making wings with your arms, and finally taking flight. In 1996, the world's biggest chicken convention took place in Ohio, USA, when about 72,000 people flocked together to do the dance. Now it's your turn to shake a tail feather!

MOONWALK

Man in the Mirror Michael Jackson (1958–2009) left audiences over the moon when he first showed his signature slide during a performance of hit single *Billie Jean* in 1983. Known as the moonwalk, this incredible optical illusion makes it appear as if you are going forwards though you are actually moving backwards. Though he didn't come up with the move himself, he brought it to the public attention. Imitation may be the sincerest form of flattery, but this one takes a lot of practice to get right.

DANCE

DANCING QUEEN

MIX UP THE MUSIC

One method of dance improvisation is to play various styles of music that you enjoy and draw on the different elements for inspiration. Don't be afraid to mix up unusual dance steps from any of the genres, from ballroom to belly dancing and tango to tap. You could end up with something completely original as a result. As well as changing the tunes, try dancing to sounds other than music. For example, listen to the sound of the wind rustling the leaves on a tree or the sound of children laughing in a park, and use the noises as your inspiration for dancing.

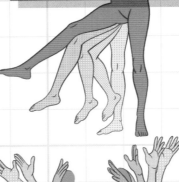

LIMBER UP

This method is all about your limbs. In front of a mirror, move your arms to the music in as many ways as you can, while keeping your legs still. Then, ensure your arms stay still as you focus on doing as many different leg movements as you can. You'll find that you don't need your whole body to come up with some great new moves.

OBJECT ASSISTANCE

Working with objects of different shapes, such as furniture, can help you find new ways to move your body. If you haven't got objects to work around, you can imagine them just as effectively. Pretend that your pillow is your partner, or imagine that you are dancing while holding a thimble full of the most precious liquid in the world – steady!

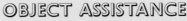

TAKE TO THE FLOOR

This one will literally wipe the floor with you! Your body interacts entirely with the floor, so choose comfy carpet or an exercise mat to prevent any injuries. You will find that when your arms and legs are restricted, you naturally involve other parts of the body in your dance, such as fingers and toes.

MAKE CHANGES

Come up with a series of simple dance steps, then look at how you can adapt them, such as changing the speed of the sequence. You could try dancing with your body as tall and stretched as possible, then try the same routine with your body low and squashed together. If you compare them in front of a mirror, you can cherry-pick your favourite moves to use again.

Welcome to the world of freestyle! When you make up your own moves on the spur of the moment without any advance choreography, it is called dance improvisation. If you're used to planning routines, this might sound a scary prospect, but coming up with a dance that is truly your own is very rewarding. As you are doing whatever moves come to mind, this type of dance is impossible to get wrong, so let go and, most importantly, have fun!

SOUNDING BOARD

Up the noise levels by turning yourself into a music machine. Use different parts of your body to make sounds, such as clapping, clicking, flicking, stamping, smacking, and tapping. Consider which sounds work best with the movement that produces them. If you find some winners, include them in your routine. However impressive your final sequence is, sound adds more interest.

TELL A STORY

Choose a character from a story you like, then improvise a dance routine where you play out the role. Wear a costume and use props to create more variety in your steps. Working with a friend is often even more fun. Together, you can come up with a story involving different characters. Try a good versus evil dance off between a fairy and a witch, improvising how they might express themselves. Just let your imagination run riot, and your body will do the rest.

> *"Switch off your mind, and move. We are born to dance."*
>
> *Dr Peter Lovatt (1964–), British psychologist and dancer*

IMAGINARY FRIEND

The concept of an imaginary friend can be useful in dance improvisation. Think about dancing with another person. Consider how their personality might influence their moves, and how you might then respond to them. If you were dancing with your friends or a stranger, alone or in a group, your routine would probably change. Try to translate these differences into your dance. Your friend need not be human either. Imagine you're flying with a flock of geese or buzzing back to a beehive to see how your body reflects these different scenarios.

YOUR SONG

Remember the song lyrics that you wrote earlier on *Word up!* (pages 26–27)? These could form the basis for your dance improvisation. Whether you went for a rap, ballad, or any other type of tune, sing the words aloud with or without accompanying music. You know your song is original, so this will help you come up with moves to match it.

TOP TIPS

- Try to free your mind and body from habits you've picked up by watching your favourite stars and copying them. This dance is all about *your* moves.
- Two heads are better than one, so invite a friend around to help with ideas. Get together, get moving, and you'll find you bounce off each other.
- Close your eyes and dance as if no one (not even you!) is watching. The best moves come when dancers stop worrying what they look like.

Even in ancient times, people loved to put on a show. While stage performances have taken place for thousands of years, the past century has seen the birth of the big screen. Today's audiences visit theatres and cinemas to see all kinds of drama, from comedy and romance to action and horror. If you long to see your name up in lights as the star of a West End production or Hollywood blockbuster, it's time to get in on the act.

DRaMa

TIME AFTER TIME

Though the concept of theatre has been around since ancient times, cinema and television are relatively recent technological advancements. The relationship between the three mediums changes over time. Sometimes they compete and conflict with each other, while at other times, they support and promote each other.

c. 15,000 BCE: Cave paintings at Lascaux, France, show figures re-enacting hunting scenes with animals. This early type of theatre may have been a way to pass on information.

7th century BCE: The Ancient Greeks perform plays and dances for entertainment. Like films today, they involve the use of scripts, sets, lighting, costumes, and actors.

c. 4th century BCE: Theatre is important in Greek society. Competitions are held in Athens, with prizes given to the best plays and performers. Some open-air amphitheatres can hold more than 15,000 people.

c. 1000 CE: A discovery by Chinese wise men becomes a breakthrough in film history. They notice that a hole in a window blind projects an upside-down picture of the scene outside. This find is later developed when Italian Girolamo Cardano (1501–76) fixes a lens into the hole, which makes the pictures clearer.

c. 1400: The church is very powerful in Europe. Stories from the Bible are performed on pageant wagons that travel around towns on holy days.

c. 1400: A highly stylized form of theatre, called Noh, begins in Japan. Originally, it lasts a whole day, and is performed by men. Masks, music, and gesture are used to tell the stories.

1576: London's first theatre is built. In 1599, it is rebuilt on the south bank of the River Thames and is called The Globe. Many of Shakespeare's plays are performed here for the first time.

1603: In Japan, a miko (spiritual guide), named Okuni, creates dance dramas in the riverbeds of Kyoto. This develops into comic plays and the arrival of kabuki – an exciting theatre form using song and dance that is still popular in Japan today.

1660: Theatres are banned in the English Civil War (1642–51). When King Charles returns to England, he brings plays back and lets women perform in them. Theatres become the places to go and be seen.

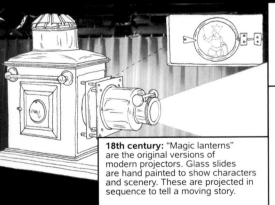

17th century: Until the middle of this century, watching plays is mainly an outdoor activity. With a move towards specially built theatres, the use of lighting and painted scenery also become more sophisticated.

17th century: The shadow theatres of Java and other Asian countries use elaborate puppets. Javanese puppets tell traditional tales with a narrator and an orchestra. Shadow puppets spread from the Far East to Europe during this century.

18th century: Travelling peep shows are very popular, especially among country people who have little or no entertainment.

18th century: "Magic lanterns" are the original versions of modern projectors. Glass slides are hand painted to show characters and scenery. These are projected in sequence to tell a moving story.

18th century: A popular form of theatre in Italy, called commedia dell'arte, has a big influence across Europe. Pantomime and Punch & Judy shows can be traced back to these traditions, which include lots of simple visual gags, such as a custard pie in the face. This is still known as "slapstick comedy".

1803: When theatre first moved indoors, light came from either flaming torches or candles. The Lyceum Theatre in London becomes the first to use gas lighting, which can be more easily controlled. Electric lighting does not appear until 1881 when the Savoy Theatre, also in London, installs a system containing 1,158 lamps that can be controlled by six dimmers.

19th century: Live horses racing! Ghosts appearing from nowhere! Train hurtling towards women tied to railway tracks! All of these happen on stage in melodramas designed to give audiences more amazing sensations. Advances in lighting, machinery, and hydraulics help with these effects.

1889: American Thomas Edison perfects a device called the Kinetograph, and uses it to make a film of a man removing his hat. Five years later, the Edison Corporation sets up the first motion-picture studio, a Kinetograph production centre called the Black Maria. The first Kinetograph parlour opens in New York, USA, where people look into a Kinetograph to see a short film.

1895: French inventor Louis Lumière creates a portable motion-picture camera and presents the first projected, moving pictures to a paying audience in Paris, France. An American called George Eastman develops a new type of film made from celluloid. He bases his film sizes on the glass photographic plates he was making before film became available. Starting with the biggest window glass he can find, he repeatedly halves the panes to make the sizes he requires. So the film used today is based on the sizes of windows in Rochester, USA, in the 19th century!

Late 19th century: French artist and inventor Emile Reynaud creates the Praxinoscope viewer. It is a device that can be used to animate sequences of still pictures by using mirrors to project them onto a screen. It is a huge success and paves the way for the cartoon animations that are popular today.

1879: Theatre audiences who had flocked to see melodramas are quickly converted to the wonders and trickery of cinema. Playwrights begin to write plays that create believable characters in realistic situations. One example is Norwegian writer Henrik Ibsen's play *A Doll's House*, which tells the story of a woman in an unhappy marriage, who shockingly for the time, leaves her husband and children to make a new life for herself.

1903: Based on the book by American author Frank Baum, *The Wizard of Oz* opens on Broadway in New York. It is shown as a musical and proves to be a big hit. The show heralds a new era of musical theatre on stage and screen.

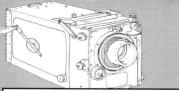

1908: The Debrie Parvo compact camera has a light wooden body. The operator starts filming by turning the crank. It is popular with film-makers for 40 years.

1910: Many film-makers and actors head west for California, USA, to a sleepy town called Hollywood. Land is cheap, and the good weather helps filming. There is a variety of landscapes to shoot in the area.

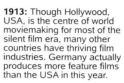

1912: In Chicago, USA, the publication *Photoplay* debuts as the first magazine for film buffs.

1913: Though Hollywood, USA, is the centre of world moviemaking for most of the silent film era, many other countries have thriving film industries. Germany actually produces more feature films than the USA in this year.

1919: Married couple Mary Pickford and Douglas Fairbanks, two of the greatest silent film stars, join Charlie Chaplin and director D W Griffith to found United Artists, now part of MGM. United Artists fund and distribute films.

1925: Scottish engineer John Logie Baird transmits a television picture in a shop in London. However, televisions did not become a common feature in homes until the 1950s.

1929: The first "talkie" films appear. Many people predict that the public will prefer silent films, but these disappear quickly. For a while, audiences flock to the cinema just to enjoy the novelty of hearing actors speaking.

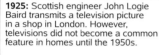

1920: Hollywood grows quickly. Studios are set up and movie legends are created. Silent screen stars become experts at expressing themselves with their faces and hands. They are rewarded with exclusive contracts and bumper salaries.

1929: The best-known film awards ceremony begins in Hollywood. The Academy Awards, or Oscars, are given annually by the United States Academy of Motion Picture Arts and Sciences for the best films, actors, directors, and many other categories.

1930: With chandeliers and carpets, cinemas become so grand that people nickname them "picture palaces". In 1930, when the population of the USA is 122 million, Americans go to the cinema 95 million times a week!

1930: As head of the Motion Picture Producers and Distributors of America, William Hays establishes a code of decency to outline what is acceptable in films.

1932: Going to the cinema is a way to escape the pressures and troubles of real life. At the same time, theatre is finding ways to discuss these same troubles and suggest ways to make life better. This is very true in Germany, where, faced with Hitler's rise to power, plays such as Bertolt Brecht's *The Mother* encourage people to fight against facism.

1930s: British studios flourish in this decade. The best-known studio, Pinewood, is founded by tycoon J Arthur Rank. The Rank Organization buys the Odeon cinema chain in 1936, which allows them to make, distribute, and show their own films.

1932: From 1900, inventors try to capture natural colours in the camera, so films are no longer only black and white. When the Technicolour company produces a "three-strip" camera, colour films are possible, but even then, they are costly and tricky to produce. By 1954, half of all films are still made in black and white.

1933: Drive-in movies begin in the car culture of New Jersey, USA. In the USSR, the government builds cinemas in railway carriages to take films to remote areas.

1935: A merger creates the famous studio 20th Century Fox. Fox Studios, one of the merged companies, pioneers both sound and colour.

1940s: This is the golden age of Hollywood, when glamorous starlets Ingrid Bergman, Bette Davis, Marlene Dietrich, Vivien Leigh, Marilyn Monroe, and Greta Garbo appear on the big screen.

1946: The Cannes Film Festival debuts in France. The most prestigious award is the Palme d'Or (Golden Palm), awarded to the best film shown during the annual festival.

1950s: With cinemas in most towns, many more people watch films than go to the theatre. There are often several cinemas in a town, showing new movies every week. The costs involved in producing a play mean theatres may stage the same play for weeks. Good plays are often turned into films and reach a wider audience.

1956: Television can be blamed for taking audiences from theatres and cinemas, but the opposite may be true. In 1956, John Osbourne's play *Look Back in Anger* attracts the attention of major theatre critics, but audiences are minimal until it is discussed on television, when it becomes a huge hit and is turned into a film with an all-star cast.

1950s: After World War II, there is a peak in popularity for non-English world cinema, in particular, Asian cinema. Many of the most critically acclaimed Asian films are produced in this decade. Japan has movie greats, such as *Seven Samurai* (1954) and *Godzilla* (1954). India produces about 200 films a year.

1960s: The studio system in Hollywood declines, partly because it becomes cheaper to film on location. Even traditional American cowboy films start to be shot in Spain and Italy, becoming known as "spaghetti Westerns". Advances in technology mean that different parts of film-making can be carried out overseas.

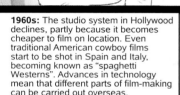

1970s: The popularity of theatre is hit by competition from cinema and television, until a new form of musical, the "rock opera", gives it second wind. British composer Andrew Lloyd Webber forms the Really Useful Group, which produces *Cats, The Phantom of the Opera,* and *Jesus Christ Superstar.*

1980s: People begin to watch films at home on video recorders. By waiting for cinema blockbusters to go to video and later DVD, they can watch them more cheaply and in the comfort of their own homes.

1980s: With more films being watched at home, the cost of running large cinemas for small audiences means that many have to shut, though many people still want to see new releases on the big screen. The solution is the multiplex – one cinema showing lots of films in smaller auditoriums.

1996: The biggest wide-screen format is IMAX. Frames ten times bigger than normal are projected onto a vast curved screen, producing a spectacular sense of realism. People visit these special cinemas for the ultimate film experience. Some screenings are 3-D (three-dimensional), and viewers must wear special glasses to see them.

2000s: Just as audiences used to flock to the cinema to see Hollywood stars on screen, more recently the desire to see big names on the live stage has resulted in an increasing number of smash films being turned into theatre spectacles, especially musicals, such as *High School Musical, Sister Act,* and *Ghost.*

LET'S GET IT STARTED

Once a film screenplay has been written, the parts are cast, the sets are constructed, and the studios are booked, filming can get under way. It takes many months and sometimes even years to make a film. When you watch a film at the cinema, you don't realize how many people and processes are involved to get it to this final stage. Sneak a peek behind the scenes of a film studio and all will be revealed. If you're ready – lights, camera, action!

ON SET

Indoor stages are permanent fixtures at film studios. They are huge areas to allow for the large sets used in film scenes. To reduce outside noise, stages have padded walls and indicator lights at the entrance. Green shows a rehearsal is under way, while red means filming is in progress. It may look like a cast of thousands are involved, but everyone has a specific role. Lighting experts check the lighting suits the scene. Directed by the cinematographer, camera operators use hand-held or free-standing cameras. The boom operator positions a large microphone to record the dialogue. The head honcho is the director, who commands all the action. When everyone is in place, filming begins. Take one!

GREENSCREEN

To save time and effort, actors often perform against a greenscreen instead of a real backdrop. The actors behave as though they are in a specific situation. The greenscreen is then later replaced in the editing suite by footage of the required scenario, so the actors can appear to be flying through Space, standing on a Formula 1 racetrack, or lost in the Sahara Desert. By the time the final film is put together, the entire scene appears to have been shot in one go because the background is combined so convincingly with the actor's scenes.

STUNT SHOOT

Action scenes in films are becoming much more advanced. If a stunt is too difficult to perform, computer-generated imagery (CGI) may be used to help create the effect. This is the safest way, as no one gets hurt. If a stunt is going to be filmed at the studio, camera crews are placed in different positions to capture the most exciting angles. Ambulances are also on standby should anything go wrong. Some actors are insured so that they can perform the stunts themselves. However, if a scene is particularly dangerous, a trained stunt double who resembles the actor will do the scene instead. The film editors will ensure the audience never notices it is not the same person by the final cut.

WATER TANK

Most film sets have a specially constructed tank for underwater scenes. Though these scenes are tricky to film, it is still much easier to film in the tank than use the sea or a river for the shoot, and be at the mercy of nature. Water is kept warm and clean, so the starlets don't complain! The director doesn't get wet, though. Instead, filming is viewed through a glass window in the tank and communication is by microphone. Wearing scuba-diving equipment, camera operators get to work inside the tank, listening to the orders from the director about which angles work best. If stormy seas are required for the scene, a wave machine creates the choppy waters.

FOLEY STUDIO

If recording a real sound is proving difficult or is simply impractical during the actual filming, sound engineers get to work in the foley studio. Here, there are thousands of props available to produce all kinds of natural sounds. A special floor area is equipped with every type of indoor and outdoor surface, so footsteps can be recreated after the actors' scenes have been shot. Banging coconut shells can sound like horses' hooves, while a cabbage being chopped in half can replicate some poor unfortunate having his arm or leg sawn off in a horror film! Later in the editing suite, these sounds must be perfectly synchronized with the action shown on screen.

EDITING SUITE

Once filming is complete, all the material goes to the editing suite to be compiled correctly. The film editor looks at the cuts on screen and makes a first draft of the film called a rough cut, putting the best shots in the right order. In the past, editors had to literally cut up pieces of film and stick them together, so that is where the name comes from. Using the rough cut, the editor trims the scenes, carefully blends them together, and adds links to ensure a smooth finish. This version is called a fine cut. Finally, the fine cut is sent to the sound department to have the soundtrack of music, dialogue, and sound effects added.

TEAM EFFORT

During filming, studios buzz with activity. There are wardrobe, hair, and make-up teams on hand to prepare the actors' costumes and get them into character. Catering crews set up tents or arrive in wagons to serve meals throughout the day. Staff run the main reception and studio offices. People called runners are on set to carry messages around the studios, while security guards monitor entrances and exits to protect the stars. Phew!

DRAMA

A STAR IS BORN

It's a long way from your bedroom to Broadway. But if you're determined to hit the big time, you'll need some help and a sprinkle of lady luck to get you there. Before you start dazzling agents with your natural talents, there are a few tricks of the trade to learn as you continue to work on your performance ability. Then, you'll be equipped with all you need for the bright lights of the big city. Make way, there's a new star in town!

SUPER SKILL SET

Working on your singing, dancing, and acting abilities, by practising every day or taking lessons with an expert, will help you to hone the skills you'll need to be a starlet. Learning other skills, such as playing an instrument or learning how to do stunts on stage, will also benefit you. Going to see lots of live theatre and reading plays will give you a broader knowledge and understanding of show business. The more tricks you have up your sleeve, the better you'll fare against all the competition.

HEALTHY LIVING

You've got to take care of yourself if you're going to be in the spotlight. A theatre actor usually wakes up very late in the morning in order to catch up on his or her sleep after the show the night before. Eight hours sleep is a minimum in this line of work to keep you fresh and bright for the routine of daily performances. A healthy breakfast is needed to provide energy for the day's work, but dairy products or citrus fruits are off the menu because they can affect the quality of your voice. Also, actors usually eat a small meal before the show to ensure energy levels don't drop during performances.

MAKE YOURSELF HEARD

Your voice must sound clear and controlled on the stage. Performers need to be able to project their voices when they are singing and speaking in order to convey meaning and emotion to the whole audience, including those sitting in the cheap seats at the back! Having the right breathing technique is essential for proper voice projection. When talking normally, people tend to use air only from the top of the lungs, but in order to truly project your voice, you need to learn how to breathe more deeply and control the flow of air through your vocal folds – see *You're the voice* (pages 18–19) for more information. Some actors go on "vocal rest", which means they try not to talk before they go on stage in order to preserve their voice.

TOP TIPS

- Audition for any theatre productions in your local community, as this is a great place to start.
- Getting a lead role in a school play will get you on the right path.
- By going to as many theatre shows as possible, you will familiarize yourself with both amateur and professional performances. If you know the productions you want to be involved in, it will help you with practice and auditions.

ALL CRIED OUT

The best actors have an ability to feel the same way that the character they are playing feels. One way they do this is to remember situations that they have personally experienced that resemble the ones their character is going through in the drama. This technique is called "affective memory". Other tricks for turning on the waterworks include rubbing mentholated balm under the eyes. It takes about a minute to work, so you need to get the preparation time right. Whatever you do, don't cut up onions backstage. They are total stinkers and your eyes will sting so much it will be hard to concentrate.

"I used to think as I looked at the Hollywood night, there must be thousands of girls sitting alone like me, dreaming of becoming a movie star. But I'm not going to worry about them. I'm dreaming the hardest."

Marilyn Monroe (1926–62),
American film star

LAUGH OUT LOUD

Laughter may be the best medicine, but faking it can be a nightmare. A good tip for laughing on stage is to get caught up in the moment. If you're properly in character, you should respond to the comedy dialogue with laughter automatically and naturally. Do consider how big the laugh should be and try to measure it accordingly. Is it just a snigger or a real guffaw? This will dictate whether you giggle momentarily or throw back your head and release a loud laugh. Also, try not to analyse the reason why things are funny too much. It is better to decide which type of laugh you're going for and then forget it, otherwise your laughter will sound forced and the audience will be unamused.

FIGHTING FIT

Choreographed violence for the stage should look realistic, and this can be a true test of acting ability. Striking a balance between fighting convincingly and not physically hurting the other person is the aim to ensure there are no serious injuries. To make a fake slap or a punch appear realistic, a sound called a knap is made. Knaps are usually produced by the actor playing the victim. For example, to give a slap, swing your hand at your partner's face. The knap is made by the victim slapping their hands together as they turn their head away. To swing a punch, move your hand towards your partner's face. The knap is made by the the victim hitting their own chest with one hand. Ouch!

EXTRA!

Don't expect to be given a lead role at the start. Most people have to begin at the bottom and work their way up. You can learn a lot by becoming involved with your local youth theatre or amateur dramatics society. By being an understudy (the second-choice actor who fills a role if the main one becomes ill or unavailable), a member of the chorus, or helping out backstage, you will gain valuable experience and get access to people who know the business inside out. Contact your local theatre to enquire about opportunities for work experience.

DRAMA

HOW TO:

- PREPARE A KIT
- MAKE LIKE A MONSTER
- FAKE A WOUND
- CRAFT A PHANTOM MASK

BRILLIANT DISGUISE

"I had no idea of the character. But the moment I was dressed, the clothes and the make-up made me feel the person he was. I began to know him, and by the time I walked onto the stage, he was fully born."

Charlie Chaplin (1889–1977), British actor

PREPARE A KIT

Put together a stage make-up kit that you can use to practise on yourself, your mates, and your family. You don't have to blow the budget, so shop around different make-up ranges to see what is best for you. The kit should contain the following beauty basics – cake foundation, rouge, eyeshadow or greasepaints in an assortment of colours, eyeliner, mascara, lipstick, lip gloss, applicator sponges, brushes, make-up remover, and tissues or wipes. Cake foundation is popular in the theatre, as it covers well and blends easily. Sponges are used to apply and blend the foundation. Several small brushes can be used to sweep eyeshadow and eyeliner around the eyes.

Be warned that some make-up can cause allergic reactions, so test items on a small area of skin first.

Grab your lipstick, powder, and paint! On stage, every character's features must be visible to the audience. Make-up can highlight facial features that might be washed out by strong stage lights. Expert make-up artists are on hand to perform all kinds of visual wizardry. Under the theatre lights, their handiwork can subtly enhance or dramatically change a starlet's features to transform them into character. Try it yourself, but don't forget remover!

70

A – tissues
B – applicator sponge
C – cake foundation
D – rouge
E – eyeshadow
F – greasepaints
G – small brushes
H – mascara
I – lipstick
J – make-up remover

TOP TIPS

- Think up new characters that you can do make-up for. Experiment with different colours and applications. Always consider the style of production, type of character, and your audience when planning the make-up to use.
- Keep checking your make-up under bright light, so you see where the light falls and which parts of the face are in shadow. This will help you work out which areas to play up with more colour.

MAKE LIKE A MONSTER

You shall go to the monsters' ball! You can vary your colours depending on whether you want to create a pale-faced vampire, a green and ghoulish Frankenstein, or a rotting zombie.

WARNING! Stage blood can stain, and it is hard to remove. If you don't have any, try mixing red food colouring with a little golden syrup.

  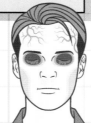  

1. Apply pale cake foundation all over the face and neck to give the skin a deathly pallor. Blend well. If the hands are on display, cover them as well.

2. Brush purple and green eyeshadow or greasepaints around the eye sockets. Use green and blue eyeliner to draw dramatic veins on the forehead.

3. Lip gloss is very good for creating a ghoulish, oozy effect. Rub some under the eyes and nose to resemble ectoplasm.

4. Use black lipliner or eyeliner to outline the lips. Then apply liberal amounts of black lipstick to contrast the pale face.

5. Drip stage blood under the eyes and at the corners of the mouth for maximum terrifying effect. The monster is ready to be unleashed!

FAKE A WOUND

In dramatic stage productions, action heroes may have to fall or fight and get injured in the process. Fake facial injuries must be highly visible to ensure they are not lost under the intensity of the lights.

If you don't have any mortician's wax, wounds and scars can be bought ready-made from specialist make-up suppliers.

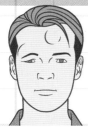 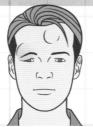 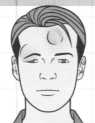 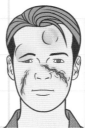 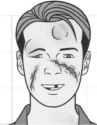

1. Mortician's wax is a soft tinted wax used for making fake injuries. It can be sculpted and applied to create swellings on the skin.

2. Once a bump is in place on the face, colour over it with rouge to suggest immediate soreness and bruising.

3. For more subtle bruising, mix purple, green, and yellow eyeshadow into the skin. Careful blending will ensure it looks authentic.

4. For open wounds, mix red food colouring into petroleum jelly, such as Vaseline. Place crumpled tissue at the wound site and cover with the mixture.

5. If the hero has been in a fist fight, tooth wax is ideal to black out teeth and turn him into a toothless wonder!

CRAFT A PHANTOM MASK

In the famous musical *The Phantom of the Opera*, the tragic phantom falls in love with the theatre's singing star, Christine. His distinctive white mask is easy to make and instantly recognizable.

   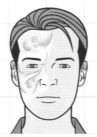 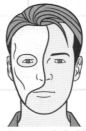

1. Get a plain white plastic mask. You can buy a cheap one at most fancy dress or joke shops.

2. Use a picture of the phantom as a reference to cut the mask across the forehead to the nose, mouth, and chin.

3. Cover one half of your face in white foundation exactly where the half mask will cover, so this area remains hidden until you remove it.

4. Mix rouge and different eyeshadows to make some of the areas on the white side appear red, bruised, and swollen.

5. Attach or simply hold the mask over your face, taking care not to smudge the make-up underneath. Wait to whip your mask off and shock your audience!

HISTORY REPEATING

Movie buffs can find themselves hooked on classics, when many of the latest blockbuster releases turn out to be imaginative treatments of plays and novels from the past. By updating the original narratives for the big screen with popular stars, sharp editing, and hit soundtracks, a new audience discovers these great works of literature for the first time.

> **"A classic is a book that has never finished saying what it has to say."**
>
> *Italo Calvino (1923–85), Italian author*

LOVE TODAY

The classic play *Romeo and Juliet* by English poet and playwright William Shakespeare (1564–1616) was completely updated in 1995 by Australian director Baz Luhrmann, who brought rock and hip-hop music to his film version. With American idols Leonardo DiCaprio and Claire Danes playing the star-crossed lovers, the film found a fresh young audience, many of whom had never read the original play. This heralded the beginning of a Shakespeare revival in a flurry of teen movies.

BARD'S REBIRTH

Young people were able to relate to American film *10 Things I Hate about You* (1999), which was an adaptation of Shakespeare's comedy *The Taming of the Shrew*. Another example of the Bard's work being given an innovative new treatment is the Walt Disney animation *The Lion King* (1994), which is a reworking of his popular play *Hamlet*, but with cartoon lions taking the leading roles, supported by a cast of other African animals!

WHAT THE DICKENS?

Many of the novels of British writer Charles Dickens (1812–70) have been turned into films and given a contemporary twist. The festive tale *A Christmas Carol*, in which three ghosts visit miserly Ebeneezer Scrooge to teach him important life lessons, has undergone a variety of different interpretations. The Muppets did a version that stayed true to the original, while the book also got the Walt Disney treatment in *Mickey's Christmas Carol*.

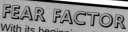

GIRLS ON FILM

Film versions of stories by British author Jane Austen (1775–1817) have brought heroines such as Elizabeth Bennet and Emma Woodhouse to the big screen. Her best-known book, *Pride and Prejudice*, has had the most adaptations. Popular romantic comedy *Bridget Jones's Diary* (2001) is also based on the novel, with Colin Firth playing a modern-day version of misunderstood Mr Darcy.

FEAR FACTOR

With its beginnings in folklore, the bites and bloodlust of vampires moved in all their gory glory from literature to film. *Dracula* (1897) by Irish author Bram Stoker has had more than 150 reworkings on film, including the silent classic *Nosferatu* (1922). In the 21st century, the *Twilight* series of vampire books and films has found a young audience to revel in the bloodsuckers all over again.

WONDERLAND

Lewis Carroll's enduring children's tale *Alice in Wonderland* (1865) tells the story of a girl named Alice who falls down a rabbit hole into a mad world of crazy characters. It has been depicted in various screen versions since the turn of the 20th century, including a silent film and a Walt Disney cartoon. In 2010, quirky film director Tim Burton revisited the book, with a 19-year-old Alice returning to the scene of her childhood adventures.

FURRY FEST

Animal magic is a popular narrative genre that has been revived on the big screen. Roald Dahl's classic for children *Fantastic Mr Fox* (1970) was given animated life in 2009 with an all-star line-up voicing the characters. Another furry feature film is *Where the Wild Things Are* (2009), an adaptation of Maurice Sendak's children's story, in which a little boy creates a world inhabited by wild creatures.

EPIC ADVENTURES

Classic tales of adventure translate well in today's computer-generated imagery (CGI) film formats. *The Lord of the Rings* was first a famous fantasy novel written by J R R Tolkien. The story was translated into different languages, becoming one of the most popular works of the 20th century. In 2001, the epic adventure was made into a film trilogy, resulting in a series of blockbusters at the box office.

WHAT'S GOING ON?

As you sit in the audience watching a show and tapping your feet, you don't see all the activity going on behind the scenes. If you want to work in the theatre, it's important to know what happens where and who does what. *(stage whisper)* Shhh, don't tell anyone. Here's your backstage pass, with access all areas...

SET DESIGN

The look of a show is determined by the set. Designers spend months planning the set with the show's director, building set models to show how they will look. Computer graphic visuals can be projected onto the set to produce moving backdrops. One show may need many different sets. In large theatres, sets can be assembled off the stage and moved on stage when needed, using hydraulic hoists or mobile platforms called dollies. Some stages are built in sections so that different parts can be raised, lowered, or revolved. A system of winches or hydraulics enables parts of the stage and set to be moved during the performance.

SET THE STAGE

From the audience's perspective, a stage may look flat, but sometimes it slopes forward slightly so that everyone can see the actors at the back of the stage. This is called a raked stage, and it is why the back of the stage is called upstage, while the front is called downstage. High above the stage, out of sight of the audience, large theatres have a grid of metal walkways and bars. These hold the stage lights and tabs (curtains), and allow part of the set, or the actors themselves, to appear to "fly" using hoists and pulleys.

BACKSTAGE

Behind, above, and below the stage, as well as in the wings (the sides of the stage), the crew move around during the show. It is their responsibility to check that all the lighting, sound, props, and set changes occur at the correct point in the performance. The stage manager coordinates the crew and the cast in order to ensure that everyone is in the right place at the right time and everything runs like clockwork.

> *"I regard the theatre as the greatest of all art forms, the most immediate way in which a human being can share with another the sense of what it is to be a human being."*
>
> Oscar Wilde (1854–1900),
> Irish author and poet

SPECIAL EFFECTS

During a show, special effects are used to make the action appear more exciting and authentic. A new generation of "intelligent" lights and lasers can produce a vast range of effects, from rain and lightning to holograms. Special fog machines can be used to pump out dry ice (frozen carbon dioxide), while pyrotechnics can create safe contained explosions or fire effects on stage. Confetti, snow, and bubbles can be produced with specialized machines. These effects may be timed to coincide with sound effects to heighten the impact.

WARDROBE

Costumes for the show are designed in advance, and once they are ready, the wardrobe department looks after them. Large theatres may have storage rooms for hats and headpieces, such as those worn by the cast of *The Lion King*. The stars of the show have private dressing rooms where they change into costume, assisted by dressers. As they must change quickly, easy fasteners such as hooks and Velcro are used instead of zips and buttons. Entire costumes may be sewn together in one piece, so the performers can slip in and out through a slit fastened with Velcro.

SOUND

The show's music and sound effects are programmed into a computer in the correct order to make a unique soundtrack. Most effects are taken from extensive prerecorded sound libraries, but some specialized sounds may have to be recorded by the theatre's sound engineer. Each effect is logged onto a cue sheet, which notes what the effect is, when it should be brought in, what volume it should be played at, and how it should be faded out. An operator starts each sound when instructed by the stage manager.

LIGHTING

As technical equipment has improved, stage lighting instruments have become more varied. Many stage lights hang on battens in front of the stage to point or focus on different areas. Basic stage lighting can illuminate characters, while specialized lighting can mark points in the plot or add atmosphere to the show. For example, blue light suggests night, while orange is sunrise. "Gobos" are metal plates that slot into stage lanterns between the lamp and lens to change the shape of the light coming out. For example, light can look like the moon or stars shining through a window.

DRAMA

UNDER PRESSURE

The stage is set for your big moment. You've been waiting for this night for many months. As you step into the light, the audience looks at you expectantly. What could possibly go wrong? The answer is, quite a lot! There are many on-stage nightmare scenarios, but more importantly, there are lots of ways to deal with these disasters to minimize the damage. Break a leg! (Don't worry, it's theatre speak for good luck!)

STAGE FRIGHT
Your heart is pounding, your hands are sweating, and your legs are shaking...

The thought of performing on the stage in front of a large audience can become overwhelming for some actors. This growing sense of anxiety can spoil the performance. There are ways to control these feelings. Never arrive late so you are rushed and thoroughly prepare your performance so that you are in complete control. Take deep breaths to calm down and do not get distracted by what is going on around you. Listen to soothing music you enjoy before going on stage. Think positive!

WARDROBE MALFUNCTION
You're up on the stage acting your heart out. Suddenly, the audience starts sniggering. You look down to see your costume has come loose revealing something very private. Eeek!

The ultimate fashion faux pas is a wardrobe malfunction. Accidentally exposing a part of your body is embarrassing at the best of times. On the stage, it's a disaster! Make sure you are very familiar with your costume. Move about in it backstage, so you know how it comes apart. Many clothes open easily for speedy costume changes between scenes. If you're worried, ask one of the wardrobe team to add a safety pin or similar to ease your fears. If the worst happens, cover up and keep on acting. The moment will soon be forgotten.

LOST VOICE
Your throat has suddenly gone dry, you swallow desperately and try to speak, but no sound comes out...

Repeated stage performances mean you run the risk of losing your voice through overuse. You should take steps to protect your lovely larynx. Try to speak as little as possible between shows to rest your voice, and avoid telephone conversations especially. Gargling with warm salt water and lemon, and drinking lots of hot tea with honey are also highly recommended. Make sure you are breathing deeply and projecting from your diaphragm, not your throat – see *You're the voice* (pages 18–19) for top tips on vocal warm-ups. On stage, don't push your voice too hard or the strain could lead to no voice at all.

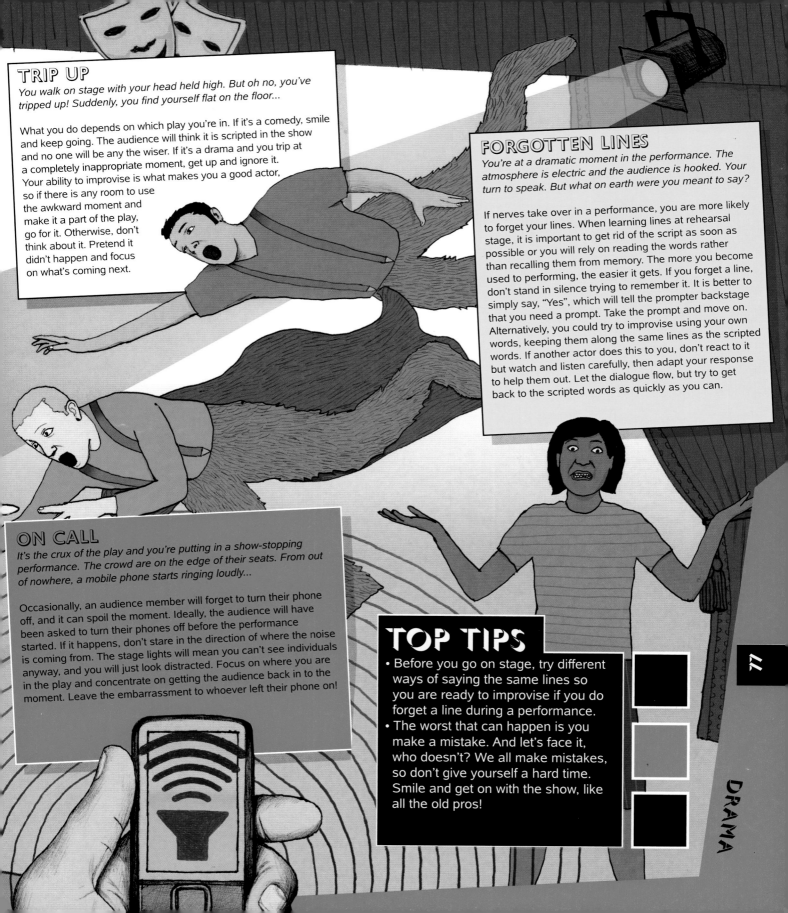

TRIP UP

You walk on stage with your head held high. But oh no, you've tripped up! Suddenly, you find yourself flat on the floor...

What you do depends on which play you're in. If it's a comedy, smile and keep going. The audience will think it is scripted in the show and no one will be any the wiser. If it's a drama and you trip at a completely inappropriate moment, get up and ignore it. Your ability to improvise is what makes you a good actor, so if there is any room to use the awkward moment and make it a part of the play, go for it. Otherwise, don't think about it. Pretend it didn't happen and focus on what's coming next.

FORGOTTEN LINES

You're at a dramatic moment in the performance. The atmosphere is electric and the audience is hooked. Your turn to speak. But what on earth were you meant to say?

If nerves take over in a performance, you are more likely to forget your lines. When learning lines at rehearsal stage, it is important to get rid of the script as soon as possible or you will rely on reading the words rather than recalling them from memory. The more you become used to performing, the easier it gets. If you forget a line, don't stand in silence trying to remember it. It is better to simply say, "Yes", which will tell the prompter backstage that you need a prompt. Take the prompt and move on. Alternatively, you could try to improvise using your own words, keeping them along the same lines as the scripted words. If another actor does this to you, don't react to it but watch and listen carefully, then adapt your response to help them out. Let the dialogue flow, but try to get back to the scripted words as quickly as you can.

ON CALL

It's the crux of the play and you're putting in a show-stopping performance. The crowd are on the edge of their seats. From out of nowhere, a mobile phone starts ringing loudly...

Occasionally, an audience member will forget to turn their phone off, and it can spoil the moment. Ideally, the audience will have been asked to turn their phones off before the performance started. If it happens, don't stare in the direction of where the noise is coming from. The stage lights will mean you can't see individuals anyway, and you will just look distracted. Focus on where you are in the play and concentrate on getting the audience back in to the moment. Leave the embarrassment to whoever left their phone on!

TOP TIPS

- Before you go on stage, try different ways of saying the same lines so you are ready to improvise if you do forget a line during a performance.
- The worst that can happen is you make a mistake. And let's face it, who doesn't? We all make mistakes, so don't give yourself a hard time. Smile and get on with the show, like all the old pros!

DRAMA

HOW TO:

YOU TOOK THE WORDS RIGHT OUT OF MY MOUTH

RHETT BUTLER

These were suave Rhett Butler's parting words to his love Scarlett O'Hara when she asked where she should go and what she should do. Imagine yourself in the part. Get yourself suited and booted, and pencil or glue a moustache on. Ensure your face is devoid of emotion, keep your voice controlled, deep, and monotone, and maintain eye contact with your leading lady. Say your piece, then walk off nonchalantly, you heartbreaker!

"Frankly, my dear, I don't give a damn!"

Rhett Butler,
played by Clark Gable in
Gone with the Wind (1939)

"Toto, I've a feeling we're not in Kansas anymore. We must be over the rainbow."

Dorothy Gale,
played by Judy Garland in
The Wizard of Oz (1939)

DOROTHY GALE

After Dorothy's tornado-flung house lands in a mystical, colourful land, she is lost and confused, but excited. Don your best blue gingham dress, put your hair in bunches, and practise looking thoroughly bewildered. Glance at your little dog Toto under your arm (a cuddly toy works just as well), then look around you and say in a sweet but worried voice the first line. Let a slow smile spread across your face as you say the second line. Eat your heart out, Judy!

JAMES BOND

Many actors have played the suave, sophisticated secret agent James Bond, and at some point, they all have to deliver this famous line. Put on your best suit, ensure your hair is looking slick, steady your gaze towards whichever baddie or leading lady you're paired up with, and introduce yourself in a calm and controlled voice. Don't forget to leave a dramatic pause after the first Bond. Very good, 007 — leave them shaken and stirred!

"... the name's Bond. James Bond."

James Bond,
played by Roger Moore,
Sean Connery, Piers Brosnan,
and Daniel Craig

"May the Force be with you."

Han Solo,
played by Harrison Ford in
Star Wars (1977)

HAN SOLO

Imagine the moment just before the Death Star battle station comes under attack. You need something special to get through this. Han Solo remains cool as a cucumber, a hero for science-fiction fans everywhere. Slip a dark waistcoat over your shirt and make your hair suitably bouffant. Turn to your chum Luke Skywalker and remind him of what matters. When you deliver the line, do it with pride and courage. Use the Force.

Classic films from past and present can have some truly memorable quotations. The screen icons featured here stole the scenes with the delivery of these corkers. Watch the films or go on YouTube to remind yourself of exactly how each line was delivered, then give your best impression by trying to re-enact them. Soon, you'll be saying, "Whose line is it anyway? I could give those stars a run for their money!"

TOP TIPS

- Don't be shy, give it a try. Play a game with your friends where they have to guess the film from the impressions you give of these characters. Try to avoid corpsing (smiling or laughing out of character).
- If you want to learn a specific accent, such as English, Irish, American, or German, listen to native speakers. You can find recordings of different accents in your library or on the Internet. Pick up on the subtleties and emphasis of different words. Try recording your attempts at the accent and play them back to hear how you sound.
- Practise, practise, practise. That's what actors have to do when they are playing a character with a strong accent or of a different nationality.

> *"I'll be back."*
> The Terminator,
> played by Arnold Schwarzenegger
> in *The Terminator* (1984)

> *"My mama always said life was like a box of chocolates; you never know what you're gonna get."*
> Forrest Gump,
> played by Tom Hanks in
> *Forrest Gump* (1994)

THE TERMINATOR

You are playing a part human, part machine sent from the future, so it doesn't get more serious than this. Grab your leather jacket, stick your shades on, and whatever you do, don't smile. Splash your face with water to give it that sweaty, busy look. The Terminator wasn't messing around when he said this. Although your eyes are not visible under your shades, your stony expression creates the mood. It's three little words, so make them strong, serious, and clearly pronounced. Hasta la vista, baby!

FORREST GUMP

A white suit, blue shirt, and white shoes will get you straight to Gumpville. Treat yourself to a box of chocolates and find a park bench (or the sofa at home) to get started. Sit down comfortably and concentrate hard. Tom Hanks hasn't won multiple Academy Awards for nothing. Speak slowly and carefully to the stranger at the other end of the bench, as if mulling over the words, and smile as you end the line. Sometimes the simplest messages have the most profound meaning, so give it your best. Now, pass the chocolates.

> *"I'm the king of the world!"*
> Jack Dawson,
> played by Leonardo DiCaprio
> in *Titanic* (1997)

> *"Speak the speech, I pray you, as I pronounced it to, trippingly on the tongue."*
> Hamlet,
> from William Shakespeare's play
> *Hamlet*, Act 3, Scene 2

JACK DAWSON

The epic film *Titanic* wasn't all doom and gloom. Though disaster would later befall the great ship on its maiden voyage, the film version of events included some fun times on board. As one of the passengers named Jack, you're a bit of a scruffbag. Mess up your hair and ensure your clothes could do with an iron. Pretend you're on the prow (front) of the ship overlooking the ocean at sunset. It's a beautiful moment, so shout the line with joy, and give plenty of air punches and whoops.

HARRY POTTER

The bewitching boy is the picture of innocence in this first film adaptation of J K Rowling's popular novels. He doesn't know exactly what's going on, but he did see the glass disappear. Put your specs on, ruffle up your hair, and add a school tie around your neck. Widen your eyes and look astonished, as you try to convince sceptical Uncle Vernon of the magic at work.

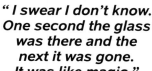

> *" I swear I don't know. One second the glass was there and the next it was gone. It was like magic."*
> Harry Potter,
> played by Daniel Radcliffe
> in *Harry Potter and the Philosopher's Stone* (2001)

> *"When you marooned me on that godforsaken spit of land, you forgot one very important thing, mate: I'm Captain Jack Sparrow."*
> Captain Jack Sparrow,
> played by Johnny Depp in
> *Pirates of the Caribbean: The Curse of the Black Pearl* (2003)

> *"I am a nice shark, not a mindless eating machine. If I am to change this image, I must first change myself. Fish are friends, not food."*
> Bruce the shark, voiced by Barry Humphries
> in *Finding Nemo* (2003)

BRUCE THE SHARK

Now this is a big ask, but all the superstars are versatile. Pretend you're an animated great white shark swimming in the ocean, making a pledge to be kinder to little fish, like Nemo. You're the boss and all the other sharks look up to you. With your flipper aloft to show the pledge, bear your gnashers and state the words in a military manner for the others to follow. If you can do this in an Australian accent, so much the better. This clear and crisp no-nonsense delivery will ensure you command respect. Let them know you're more considerate than that naughty Jaws ever was.

JACK SPARROW

This popular sea dawg knows how to deliver a funny one-liner, and now it's your turn. When he comes face to face with old enemy Captain Hector Barbossa at sea one dark night, he lets him know what a mistake he made in undermining the pirate king. A pirate hat, scrappy hair, and lots of eye make-up will help you shine, swashbuckler. As if to a captive audience, speak quietly but confidently and clearly enunciate your words. Pause after you say "mate", and smile as you remind him of who you are. Keep the comedy element, but don't forget that this line is a warning and he should pay heed.

THAT'S ENTERTAINMENT

Some films are so good they never go out of fashion. Movie buffs may criticize their content as out of date and irrelevant compared to the latest new releases, yet audiences continue to come back to them. From naughty monsters to magic nannies, and cartoon animation to live action, true classics can capture the hearts of young people around the world and across the generations.

MARY POPPINS (1964)

Directed by: Robert Stevenson
Produced by: Walt Disney
Starring: Julie Andrews as Mary Poppins, Dick Van Dyke as chimney sweep Bert
Synopsis: Based on the books by P L Travers, Mary Poppins is an English nanny with superpowers who enchants the children in her care and strives to put wrong things right before flying away when the wind changes.
Memorable moments: *Supercalifragilisticexpialidocious* – a nonsense song that Mary teaches the children.
Blockbuster because: Magical musical with an Oscar-winning Best Original Score and Best Actress performance for the leading lady. Blends live action with animation to create a dream-like feel and charming story.

GREASE (1978)

Directed by: Randal Kleiser
Produced by: Robert Stigwood and Allan Carr
Starring: Olivia Newton-John as Sandy, John Travolta as Danny
Synopsis: This romantic comedy was set in the 1950s, with good girl Sandy falling for the cool leader of the gang, Danny, during a holiday romance. Things don't go to plan when they find themselves at high school together, but in the end, love is triumphant.
Memorable moments: Duets between Danny and Sandy, such as *Summer loving* and *You're the one that I want*.
Blockbuster because: The super-catchy soundtrack has audiences singing along.

> *"Pick up a camera. Shoot something. No matter how small, no matter how cheesy, no matter whether your friends and your sister star in it. Put your name on it as director. Now you're a director. Everything after that you're just negotiating your budget and your fee."*
>
> James Cameron (1954–),
> Canadian film director

SNOW WHITE AND THE SEVEN DWARFS (1937)

Directed by: Various
Produced by: Walt Disney
Starring: Snow White and the Seven Dwarfs!
Synopsis: This American animated film is based on the German fairy tale first published by the Brothers Grimm. When a princess escapes her nasty stepmother, the queen, she goes to live with a group of seven adorable dwarfs before she meets her prince.
Memorable moments: The dwarfs singing *Heigh-ho* as they go off to work in the mines.
Blockbuster because: It was the first full-length animated feature in motion-picture history, the first produced in full colour, and the first produced by Walt Disney. Phew!

E.T. (1982)

Directed by: Steven Spielberg
Produced by: Steven Spielberg
Starring: Henry Thomas as Elliot, ET (Extraterrestrial) as himself!
Synopsis: Fantasy about a young boy who encounters a lost alien and shows him the wonders of life on Earth before helping him get home.
Memorable moments: The bicycle scene when ET uses his special powers to take himself and Elliott flying into the sky.
Blockbuster because: It's a feel-good film about friendship, completely unlike any film before it.

HARRY POTTER AND THE SORCERER'S STONE (2001)

Directed by: Chris Columbus
Produced by: David Heyman
Starring: Daniel Radcliffe as Harry Potter, with Rupert Grint and Emma Watson as his friends
Synopsis: Based on J K Rowling's adventure novel, Harry Potter learns that he is a wizard on his 11th birthday, and is sent to Hogwarts School of Witchcraft and Wizardry to start his education.
Memorable moments: Harry playing the wizard sport quidditch in which two teams of seven players ride around on broomsticks, trying to catch a ball called the Golden Snitch.
Blockbuster because: One of the best-selling novels ever becomes one of the biggest-grossing films ever, keeping both the magic and the message that good triumphs over evil.

JURASSIC PARK (1993)

Directed by: Steven Spielberg
Produced by: Kathleen Kennedy, Gerald R Molan, Steven Spielberg
Starring: Sam Neill, Laura Dern, and Jeff Goldblum as a renowned paleontologist (fossil-remains expert), a paleobotanist (fossil-plants expert), and a mathematician respectively.
Synopsis: A power cut at a theme park causes the security systems to fail, resulting in cloned dinosaurs escaping from their enclosure and causing chaos.
Memorable moments: A very angry Tyrannosaurus rex bearing down on a jeep at high speed!
Blockbuster because: The animatronics and digital animation brought the dinosaurs to life in the most realistic depiction to date.

SHREK (2001)

Directed by: Andrew Adamson, Vicky Jenson
Produced by: Jeffrey Katzenberg at DreamWorks Animation
Starring: A big, green lovable ogre named Shrek, the love of his life, Princess Fiona, and a very chatty donkey.
Synopsis: In this animated fairy tale, Shrek finds his life invaded by various storybook characters, including three little pigs and a big bad wolf, who have been thrown out of their land by evil Lord Farquaad. Shrek sets out to rescue Princess Fiona, who has been lined up to marry Farquaad, and falls for her himself.
Memorable moments: Donkey steals the show with his endless singing and joking.
Blockbuster because: The animation and humour are an award-winning combination.

TOY STORY (1995)

Directed by: John Lasseter
Produced by: Ralph Guggenheim, Bonnie Arnold
Starring: Woody the cowboy, Buzz Lightyear the spaceman
Synopsis: In this computer-animated film, a toy cowboy is mightily unimpressed when a super spaceman toy replaces him as number one in his owner's affections, and so the two become rivals.
Memorable moments: When the toys show evil adolescent Sid that they are not inanimate objects and he shouldn't mess with them.
Blockbuster because: This was the first feature film to be created entirely with CGI (computer-generated imagery). The incredible 3-D (three-dimensional) effect was ideal for the comedy mix of characters.

THE SHOW MUST GO ON

Never give up if you want to succeed in theatre or film. Be prepared for lots of auditions and castings, most of which will result in rejections. But for every 100 rejections, you might just land a part. Then you'll be busy learning lines, going to rehearsals, taking part in publicity campaigns, and before you know it, opening night is here. Afterwards come the reviews and interviews. Sigh! There really is no business like show business!

PREPARATION

Researching and practising your part is essential for any audition. Ensure you know the story very well, and familiarize yourself with your character. If there are any existing film or television adaptations, watch them to get inspiration for the role. It is not just your acting skills that will come under scrutiny. Your interpretation of the character's personality is just as important, so think carefully before you decide how to play it. Learn your monologue or dialogue, so you know the words inside out and back to front. Perform to your family and friends. The more practice runs, the better.

AUDITIONS

Hopefully, you already resemble the character to some extent, and the hair and make-up teams can do the rest should you get the part. If not, it doesn't hurt to adapt your look to suit the character you're going for. At the audition, be prepared for the casting director to ask you to repeat the performance in a different way, or read another section of the script, which is called "cold reading". The director may be throwing you in at the deep end to see how you cope, so just give it your best shot. If other people are sitting with the casting director, don't be inhibited – you'll perform in front of a lot more people should you get the part. At the end, thank the casting director for the opportunity.

REHEARSALS

Congratulations, you've got the part! Now the hard work begins. Before each rehearsal, the director will let you know which scenes you will be running through, so you can prepare for them in advance. The director is often very passionate about the play or film script, and if you know it well, this will help you to discuss the story and how it might be performed. By staying informed, you'll come across better during rehearsals. Highlight your words on your script so you don't lose track of where you are in the early rehearsals. Learn the lines properly as soon as you can, then you won't need the script.

PUBLICITY CAMPAIGNS

In the run-up to a new theatre production or film release, the publicity campaign usually goes into overdrive. Without people hearing about it, there could be low audience figures and a loss of money. As one of the cast, you may be included in media promotions. Poster advertising often features group shots of the cast, while magazines and newspapers may request photoshoots and interviews with the stars. There are also standees — big free-standing cardboard displays of film and theatre stars, usually found in cinema foyers or theatre lobbies to help the promotion. Don't panic over all the attention. Photographers will let you know how to pose for any publicity, so just relax and go with it. Smile and be friendly in interviews, but give short answers and focus on the team production rather than your individual performance.

> "There is no spray can called 'Instant Stardom', only talent can keep you at the top."
>
> *Jim Dale (1935–),*
> *British actor*

OPENING NIGHT

Whether it's a film premiere or a theatre production's first night, don't give in to the nerves. Either way, this is your chance to see the fruits of your labour. At a film premiere, the hard work is over. Sit back and relax during the screening. If any of your scenes make you feel uncomfortable, be glad the premiere is in the dark, so no one can see your reactions. If it's your first night performing at the theatre, expectations will be high. Remember everything you've learned, stay in character, and check out *Under pressure* (page 76–77), so you are equipped to deal with any on-stage disasters should they arise.

REVIEWS

After the premiere or opening night, critics will write their reviews online or in the print media. There will always be mixed reviews. While you hope for positive feedback, there is bound to be someone ready to criticize. This is all part of show business, and the longer you're involved, the more thick skinned you'll become. If your own performance comes under scrutiny, remember the saying, there's no such thing as bad publicity. The fact that people are writing about it at all will keep the show or film in the public interest. If you find your confidence knocked, keep your chin up and keep going. Many stars don't read reviews at all, so they can avoid getting upset or angry about them.

TOP TIPS

- Always be punctual, whether it's for an audition, a rehearsal, or a performance. This shows you are reliable and want to be taken seriously. It also means you don't arrive like a dart in a dartboard, but instead, cool as a cucumber.
- Acting classes can help you with auditions and make you feel more at ease in this stressful environment.
- Listen carefully to the director and do your best to follow instructions.

MY FAVOURITE MISTAKE

Today's slick film edits should result in the final cut being perfect. However, this is not always the case. Mistakes do happen. Whether they are clangers made by the cast, crew members caught accidentally on camera, or timing and continuity problems, some of the biggest blockbusters have included the silliest slip-ups. They may go unnoticed on first viewing, but once you know what to look for, it's fun spotting the film flaws.

CLANGERS

To the amusement of film buffs everywhere, clangers that should have been cut from a film are sometimes left in. It could be as literal as a cast member tripping up, but often these clangers are anachronisms. Ever seen a caveman wearing a watch? Or one of King Arthur's knights pulling out a sub-machine gun in a jousting contest? When things are shown that come from a different period in time, they are called anachronisms. These may be deliberately used in comedies to make people laugh, but they may appear in films by accident either because someone wasn't paying attention during the edits or because reshooting the scene would have been too costly.

STAR WARS

Science-fiction fans are very protective of the original *Star Wars* trilogy, but even they must have had a chuckle at the clumsy Stormtrooper in the first film. When the Stormtroopers burst into the control room, one on the right of the screen bangs his head on the hatchway! Ouch. In the sequel, *The Empire Strikes Back* (1980), Han Solo's chum Chewbacca is seen running away, with his furry feet wearing trainers! Chewie was obviously the trendiest Wookiee around.

GLADIATOR

Ancient Rome was brought back to life in the award-winning, budget-busting *Gladiator* (2000), but with a couple of surprises. At the Battle of Carthage scene in the Colosseum, one of the Roman chariots flips over to reveal a gas cylinder in the back. The gas cylinder was used to flip the chariot, but that's no excuse! The vapour trail of an aircraft in the sky can also be seen in the film – to wait until it had evaporated would have slowed down the shoot and pushed up the cost.

TITANIC

As the lovers get to know each other on board the ship in *Titanic* (1997), Jack tells Rose that he used to go ice-fishing in Lake Wissota, a man-made lake in Wisconsin, USA, where he grew up. She might have fallen for it hook, line, and sinker, but history tells us that the lake was filled with water only in 1918, when a power company built a dam there. That was six years after the ship sank, so Jack can't have had many catches of the day!

THE WIZARD OF OZ

At the beginning of children's classic *The Wizard of Oz*, Dorothy (Judy Garland) is walking on the farm when she falls in the pigpen. Luckily, Bert is on hand to help pull her out, but her dress is clean and spotless. Hmm... they made a pig's ear of that scene. What a stinker!

WANDERING CREW

Sometimes, you just can't get the staff. The crew are meant to stay off camera and ensure that everything on set goes to plan. However, with different camera operators recording from a variety of angles, the crew may get caught by one of the cameras and included accidentally in the final film cut. The outfits worn by the crew are often anachronisms in themselves, completely at odds with the period the film is meant to be showing!

PIRATES OF THE CARIBBEAN

In *The Curse of the Black Pearl*, Captain Jack Sparrow (Johnny Depp) and his motley crew find themselves a man up on board the ship. It doesn't look like a pirate, though, arrr! No, this landlubber is a crew member staring out to sea. The sunglasses and cowboy hat he was wearing were not the norm in the 17th century either. Shiver me timbers!

GLADIATOR

Maximus (Russell Crowe) is the hero of epic production *Gladiator*, and even he had to contend with modern-day pretenders trying to steal the moment. As the main man goes to see his horse, a crew member in blue jeans is seen in the background trying to duck out of the way. Too late, mate! You're in the final version, and Maximus isn't happy.

> **"There are no mistakes or failures, only lessons."**
>
> *Denis Waitley (1933–),*
> *American author*

CONTINUITY ERRORS

When you watch a film, the action moves along seamlessly. Films are not usually shot in this way, though. They are filmed in very small sections that are later edited together. Each scene may be shot many times as the director tries to get the best camera angle, the best lighting, and the best performances from the cast. Every time a scene is shot, it is called a "take". A continuity person is hired to make sure that every time a scene is reshot, everything looks exactly the same. It is their job to make detailed notes and take digital photographs of how the set and characters look on each take. If this goes well, the audience will think the whole film sequence was recorded in one go. If it goes wrong, this can happen...

TOP GUN

In 1986, *Top Gun* shot up the film chart as audiences fell for the fighter pilots competing to be the best of the best! One cheesy scene towards the end saw Maverick (Tom Cruise) being lifted onto the shoulders of the other boys. As he goes up, he's not wearing sunglasses, but on the way down, the sunnies are on!

TOMB RAIDER

Adventure flick *Tomb Raider* (2001) starred everyone's favourite action girl Lara Croft (Angelina Jolie), but even her abilities were surpassed by supporting character Alex West (Daniel Craig), who managed to be in two places at once! During the dramatic raid on the tomb, he's in the thick of the action, helping a group of people who are pulling on ropes to open the tomb. In the next second, he is stood at the front by the tomb entrance. Now that's quick work!

LORD OF THE RINGS

Fantasy adventure *The Lord of the Rings* (2001) was a film on an epic scale, but it did not always pay attention to detail. The scar on young hobbit Frodo Baggins (Elijah Wood) doesn't stay still. It starts off on his lower right cheek, near to his chin, but it then repeatedly changes size and position throughout the rest of the film. Hobbits may be imaginary creatures (with hairy feet), but this continuity error is very real!

HARRY POTTER

In *Harry Potter and the Sorcerer's Stone* (2001), sorcerer Harry (Daniel Radcliffe) is seen at the start-of-term feast. Initially, he is sitting next to Ron Weasley (Rupert Grint), but when the food comes, he is suddenly on the other side of the table next to Hermione Granger (Emma Watson). Could it be magic from the boy wonder or, more likely, just another continuity error?

HOW TO:

- WRITE A SCRIPT
- DO STORYBOARDS
- CREATE DIALOGUE
- MAKE MOVIE MAGIC

EVERY PICTURE TELLS A STORY

WRITE A SCRIPT

A document that includes the writer's ideas on everything that should be seen and heard by an audience is called a script. By the time a director and production crew have agreed to take on a script, they may make some changes to it. This is a normal part of the process. If you aspire to screenwriting, watch lots of films and television programmes to get more ideas. Also, read through screenplays so you can see the format and style used by screenwriters. You can look on the Internet for standard conventions regarding the document layout and font (typeface), but you don't need to worry about those details just yet.

DO STORYBOARDS

Don't forget that film is a visual medium. Always picture how your words will be translated on a screen format. Scripts are not read as you might read a novel or story, so write what you want the audience to see and hear. Storyboards can help with this process, especially if you are more of a visual thinker than a writer. Similar to a comic, storyboards consist of a series of rough images used to outline the plot. The key moments in a story or an action sequence can be sketched out for clarity, helping you to visualize them in your own mind.

Whenever you watch your favourite television programme, go to the cinema, or play a computer game, you are seeing the work of a scriptwriter. It may seem easy because of how well shows and films are put together, but penning a blockbuster is a big challenge. If you want to have a go, it's going to take time and effort. Very few scriptwriters sell their first drafts, and many of them take years to perfect their masterpiece.

TOP TIPS

- Keep revising the screenplay before you send it to a production company. It's got more chance of being a success once you are truly happy with it.
- Ask family and friends to read your script, as you are more likely to get honest opinions. Tell them that you are not looking for specific criticism, but overall thoughts on whether the plot and structure work.

CREATE DIALOGUE

This may be the first time you've tried to write dialogue. The best advice to make it sound realistic and convincing is to pay attention to people talking around you. Novels usually consist of lengthy description, but in reality, people usually shorten their expressions in everyday conversation. Listen to the phrases they use and model your writing on them. Try to avoid clichéd language and, instead, make sure each one of your characters has a particular style of speaking that is unique to them. As a writer, you need to be clear about the story (what happens) and the plot (why it happens). Decide what the characters are like and why they do what they do. Once you have this clear in your head, the dialogue will flow more naturally. Don't be in a rush to start writing dialogue, as this can come later.

MAKE MOVIE MAGIC

First things first, what makes a good film? Here is a list of main points for you to consider before writing your screenplay, and if you manage to include them all, you could be on to a winner!

GENRES

Choose your genre. Whether it is horror, action, or romance, you should know what your genre is and, as a result, the type of audience you are appealing to. If you are struggling, the age-old advice is to write about what you know and, more importantly, what you care about. This will make you write with conviction. So if you want to write an epic war film, but your experiences to date are more about home and school life, see if you can write a family film more convincingly.

MEANING

The big question to start with is, what is the point of your film? What is the reason you are writing it? This doesn't mean it has to be a big moral lesson for everyone to learn from, but in some way, your story must try to say something that the audience can recognize and relate to.

GOALS

Good films usually give the lead character a goal or aim. It could be winning a race, landing a job, or saving the planet, but there should be a lot riding on it, and the audience must share the sense of how important it is. For it to really matter, the audience must believe it matters.

CHARACTERS

When characters are well developed, it makes the audience care about them. This doesn't just mean the heroes and heroines of your screenplay. Villains can create just as much feeling. The audience want to feel as much for the characters as you did creating them, and once you've got the audience on side, your screenplay has a greater chance of success.

IMAGINATION

You may want to write a story that you couldn't possibly have any first-hand experience of, such as a piece of science fiction. This is fine, but remember that even in fantasy worlds, the characters (human or otherwise!) still have hopes, fears, and relationships, and these are what your audience will relate to.

"You must write your first draft with your heart. You rewrite with your head. The first key to writing is to write, not to think."

William Forrester (Sean Connery), from the film *Finding Forrester* (2000)

83

CONFLICT

Though most of us avoid conflict in real life, we welcome it in films and television. Without conflict, goals are too easily achieved by lead characters and the story is less interesting. One of the main reasons why we watch drama is to see how characters deal with the challenges they face.

STRUCTURE

The structure of most screenplays tends to have a clear beginning, middle, and end. Key events will fall within these sections to signpost the audience through the story. It is important to note down what will happen and when within these three parts, so the plot is set.

CLIMAX

The screenplays of many box-office smashes build up to a dramatic point just before the end. This is the biggest scene in the film and potentially the highlight. At this moment, the character fights against good, evil, or perhaps a personal character flaw. The struggle and resolution stands out as the film's climax and conclusion.

REWRITING

Expect to keep rewriting your screenplay. You may have a spate of writing reams of notes, but your screenplay needs to be revisited repeatedly. Keep checking your story, structure, and dialogue, looking for ways to improve it. Editing is essential.

THE FAME

Whether you're a singing star, a dancing diva, or a screen dream, playing the fame game isn't easy. It's tough at the top. You love the perks of being a VIP, but you want to keep your privacy. You need the media spotlight, but you can't always know what they'll say about you. You're a good egg most of the time, but pressure can bring out the worst in you. Fame is a balancing act between staying in the public eye and protecting your private persona.

REMEMBER YOUR ROOTS

Never forget where you came from. Your friends and family have always been there, so don't let your relationships slide as you board the first flight to Hollywood! When people become famous, their egos can expand so their personalities become unrecognizable. All this adulation can make it hard to keep your feet on the ground, but don't lose sight of the fact that fame is often fleeting. Who will you turn to if it all falls apart? Your friends and family, of course, rather than those hangers-on who just want a slice of your showbiz action.

> *"I awoke one morning and found myself famous."*
>
> Lord Byron (1788–1824), British poet

APPRECIATE YOUR FANS

We've all been there. With a poster of our favourite starlet on the bedroom wall, we've longed for a sighting or an autograph. Don't forget that when people join your fan club, come to see your shows, and wait in the rain just to catch a glimpse of you – that was you once upon a time. Be sure to stop for a photograph, a brief chat, or even just to flash a smile. It only takes a moment, but it means a lot to your fans. And where would you be without them?

MOOD MANAGEMENT

Your schedule's a nightmare. You're going here, there, and everywhere. Everyone wants a piece of you. It's tempting to throw a strop and declare that you can't take anymore! Most celebrities who are known for their mood-monster moments are not well liked. You don't have to be superhuman, but just being human helps. Mention why you're stressed – you've had a bad-hair day, your dog's not well, or you're just a bit under the weather. The more normal you are, the more people will appreciate your honesty and, as a result, relate and warm to you. No one likes a prima donna!

MEDIA MADNESS

The media can build you up, but they can knock you down just as quickly. It's not always easy to keep them onside, but being consistent helps. If you court publicity and play up to the press, photographers and interviewers will assume you're fair game. If you want to stay out of the spotlight, avoid celeb haunts and never talk about your private life. You need the media to up your profile if you're releasing a single, doing a performance, or starring in a show, but don't depend on them. When they've had enough of you, you'll soon know about it. Don't worry – you'll learn to take the rough with the smooth.

15 MINUTES OF FAME

As American artist Andy Warhol (1928–87) said, "In the future, everyone will be famous for 15 minutes." Fame can come and go, so make the most of it. Instead of focusing on the pitfalls, look at the positives. If you're travelling the world, try to do some exploring. If you're going to glittering events, savour the moment. If you're winning awards, be proud and show that you're grateful. If you're being interviewed by a glossy magazine, relish the fact that people want to know what you're up to. These are memories for later life when you're grey and old, and nobody's interested anymore!

SONG TITLES

GLOSSARY

AMPHITHEATRE
Amphitheatres usually have semi-circular tiers of seats allowing the audience to look down on the performance area. These were popular for staging public spectacles in Ancient Greece and Rome.

ANACHRONISM
Something that is out of place, such as a person or an object, which appears in the wrong historical period.

ANIMATION
The process of making still images appear to move.

ANIMATRONICS
The use of electronics and robotics to create mechanical puppets.

AUDITORIUM
The part of a theatre where an audience watches and listens to a performance.

BALLAD
A popular slow song of a romantic sentiment, made up of verses and a repetitive chorus.

BLOG
An online journal where people can record their diary entries for others to read.

BROADWAY
The popular theatre district of New York, USA.

BUTOH
An experimental modern Japanese dance.

CASTING
The selection of actors or performers for a show.

CELLUOID
Motion-picture film.

CHORD
A group of notes combined according to a given system and usually sounded together.

CHOREOGRAPHER
A person who invents sequences of dance moves, usually to music.

CINEMATOGRAPHER
A person in charge of shooting a film.

COVER
A new version of an existing song by a different artist.

CUNEIFORM
The earliest known script, written on clay tablets in wedge-shaped characters.

DEMO
A piece of recorded music that is played to people for demonstration purposes.

DIAPHRAGM
The thin muscle skin below the chest, which pulls air into the lungs.

DOMBA
A ritual chain dance practised by young Venda women in South Africa.

DUET
A composition for two musicians or two singers.

ECTOPLASM
A smoky substance in which a dead spirit supposedly manifests itself before oozing from the body of a psychic. Many of the 19th-century cases of ectoplasm were proven to be fake, with different materials used instead.

EN POINTE
In ballet, standing on the tips of the toes.

FINGERBOARD
The part of a stringed instrument against which the fingers press the strings to vary the pitch.

FLAPPER
A fashionable woman from the 1920s who performed dances such as the Charleston in public.

FLYER
A small leaflet used to promote something, such as a new band or event.

FOLEY
The process of adding sound effects to a film at the post-production stage.

FOSSE
Named after choreographer Robert "Bob" Fosse (1927–87), this style of dance focuses on unusual parts of dancers' bodies, such as the stomach and shoulders, to create new moves.

FREESTYLE
An innovative performance by a singer or dancer that uses creativity to make original words or movements.

FRET
One of a series of ridges on the fingerboard of a stringed instrument.

GREENSCREEN
A blank green screen that actors perform in front of, when background scenes are going to be added to the film later.

HAMSTRING
A tendon in the leg that is easily overstretched, resulting in injury.

HESSIAN
A coarse, heavy fabric.

HORNPIPE
A lively British folk dance often associated with sailors of the 16th century.

HYDRAULICS
A branch of physics that looks at the practical application of liquid in motion, such as its use in hoisting parts of sets and stages in the theatre.

ICON
Somebody who has had a lasting career in the entertainment industry and, as a result, is held in high regard.

IMPROVISATION
The process of writing music, performing a dance, or playing an instrument spontaneously, without any advance planning of the composition or routine.

INSTRUMENTAL
A musical composition without any vocals or lyrics.

KABUKI
A traditional Japanese dance drama that is still popular in Japan today.

KARAOKE
A type of interactive entertainment in which amateur singers use a microphone to sing to popular recorded music, with their voice replacing the original artist's recording.

KIMONO
A loose robe worn traditionally by the Japanese.

LARYNX
The space in the throat where the vocal chords are contained.

LIP-SYNCH
A technical term for the process of matching mouth movements to recorded speech or song.

LYRICIST
A writer who specializes in producing song lyrics.

MEDLEY
Multiple pieces of music grouped together in one composition.

MELODRAMA
A film or play with sensationalized action and dialogue.

MELODY
An agreeable succession of singular musical sounds.

MIKO
A Japanese female shaman or medium who passed messages from the gods and who currently serves in shrines.

MUCUS
A thick secretion produced by people in the nose or airways that can build up in the throat and cause infection.

MUSICAL
A popular Western form of theatre, including songs and dance.

NOH
A powerful form of Japanese dance drama.

PANTOMIME
A form of festive theatre based on traditional tales, stereotyped roles, and slapstick jokes.

PAPARAZZI
Photographers who take pictures of famous people and sell them for large sums of money.

PICK
A piece of plastic that can be used instead of a thumb to pluck a stringed instrument.

PITCH
The degree of highness or lowness of a sound.

PROJECTOR
Equipment used to project films onto a surface.

PUNCH AND JUDY
A traditional puppet show at the seaside, starring Mr Punch and his long-suffering wife, Judy.

PYROTECHNICS
The art of making fireworks.

REALISM
The concern for reality and rejection of things that are considered imaginary.

RECITAL
A musical performance.

RHYTHM
The flowing pattern of movements, sounds, and images.

RIFF
A repeated section of music in rock or jazz.

ROMANTICISM
Dominating the 19th century, this musical style was inspired by a need to escape the classical conventions of the time.

SCREENPLAY
The script of a film, including decriptions, details, dialogue, and directions.

SHADOW PUPPETRY
A form of entertainment in which figures are lit from behind so their shadows are cast on a thin screen between them and the audience.

SLAPSTICK
A style of comedy that uses basic humour and silly scenarios to amuse the audience.

SOLFÈGE
An 11th-century system to help singers remember their vocal exercises.

SOUNDTRACK
The recorded music that accompanies a film.

SQUARE DANCE
A folk dance for groups of four couples, with the movements sung out by a caller.

STANDEE
The freestanding cardboard displays of film and theatre stars, usually found in shops and theatres to assist with promotion.

STORYBOARD
A series of sketches showing the scenes planned for a television programme or film.

SYMPHONY
A musical composition for a full orchestra, usually made up of four sections.

TAKE
A single shoot of a scene. The number of takes increases every time the same scene is reshot.

TANBUR
A long-necked, two-stringed instrument used mainly by musicians during the 7th and 8th centuries.

TARTAN
A cloth with a design of checks and stripes. Each pattern represents a different Scottish clan.

TONE
The pitch, quality, and strength of a musical sound.

TROUBADOUR
A strolling musician from the Middle Ages who sang songs about love.

TROUPE
A group of touring actors, singers, or dancers.

UNDERSTUDY
A person who studies a part in a play so that they are ready to step into the regular performer's role if they are unavailable for any reason.

VIP
Meaning a very important person, this term describes someone of great influence or fame who is given special treatment.

INDEX

CREDITS

DK would like to thank:

Stephanie Pliakas for proofreading, Jackie Brind for the index, and Agency Rush.

The publisher would like to thank the following for their kind permission to reproduce their photographs:

(Key: a–above; b–below/bottom; c–centre; f–far; l–left; r–right; t–top)

Alamy Images: Claudia Adams/Danita Delimont 49cr (stilts); AF Archive 13fcra, 25br, 29tr, 73tc, 73cla, 73cra, 80cl; Angela Hampton Picture Library 82c; Archives du 7ème Art/Photos 12 13crb, 51cl; Michael Ayre 41cr; BE&W agencja fotograficzna Sp. z o.o. 69cra; Nathan Benn 13ftr; blickwinkel/Schmidbauer 43bl; Chrisstockphotography 13cr; Robert Clayton 48–49 (background); Disney Enterprises Inc./Archives du 7ème Art/Photos 12 72crb; Walt Disney/Pictorial Press Ltd 72bc; Everett Collection Inc. 50cl; Eye Risk 81tc; Blaine Harrington III 39cl; Laurence Heyworth/ Montagu Images 42ca; Peter Horree 38cr; Juniors Bildarchiv/F368 69bl; Keystone Pictures USA 68bl; Nathan King 12br; Christa Knijff 42bl; KPA Honorar & Belege/United Archives GmbH 84tr; Lebrecht Music and Arts Photo Library 13fclb, 39tr; Yadid Levy 38clb; LondonPhotos – Homer Sykes 58cra; Mere Punk News 28br; David L. Moore – OR10 59c; Moviestore Collection Ltd 72bl, 84crb, 84bc; Daryl Mulvihill 15cr;

Network Photographer 43bc; Odile Noel/Lebrecht Music and Arts Photo Library 51fcra; Oasis/Photos 12 38br; Paramount/Pictorial Press Ltd 39clb; PCN Black/ PCN Photography 55cla; Pictorial Press Ltd 12bl, 12fcrb, 24cr, 25clb, 25bc, 84ca; Retro Kitsch 50c; John Sundlof 51tl; Synthetic Alan King 33ftl; Luca Tettoni/ Robert Harding Picture Library Ltd 38fcra; Universal/ Pictorial Press Ltd 80crb; Walt Disney/AF Archive 80bc, 81bl; Julie Woodhouse 12cb. **The Art Archive:** W. Langdon Kihn/NGS Image Collection 43c. **Corbis:** Bettmann 65tc; Christophe Boisvieux 43tl; Adam Burn/ fstop 10; Anna Carnochan/Retna Ltd 43cra; Demetrio Carrasco/JAI 15br; Beau Lark 36–37; John Lund/Blend Images 59tc, 59tr; Lawrence Manning 13cl; moodboard 32l; Ocean 49tc; Robert Patrick/Corbis Sygma 42c; RD/Leon/Retna Digital/Retna Ltd 47tl; Sunset Boulevard 65tr; Takeshi Takahashi/Amanaimages 43tr. **Dorling Kindersley:** Budapest Opera House 39tc; Freed of London 51bl; Judith Miller/Ancient Art 12ftr. **Dreamstime.com:** 350jb 33bl (tickets); Azham Ahmad 55crb; Bill Fehr 83tl; Milosluz 83bl; Sahua 83c. **Fotolia:** draganm 7tc, 7tr; Pei Ling Hoo 88–89; malko 6tr, 6crb; Kirsty Pargeter 6–7b, 7cla, 88–89b; Николай Григорьев 69br. **Getty Images:** AFP Photo/John Hogg 74–75; Mark Dadswell 55br; DEA/G. Dagli Orti 64tc; Phil Dent/Redferns 59bc, 59br, 59fbr; Digital Vision 14cl, 14bl; Digital Vision/Thomas Northcut 68br; Javier Fernandez Del Corral/WireImage 39fcbr; Gallo Images/ Latitudestock 64cl; Gallo Images/Martin Harvey 15tr; General Photographic Agency 65fcra; Hola Images 48tr; Hulton Archive 12fcra, 58bc, 64bl; Image Source 40bl; Dimitrios Kambouris/WireImage for Tony Awards 47cr; Kean Collection 38bl; Mike Kemp 49cr, 49bc; Junko Kimura 64cra; Kevin Mazur/WireImage for *New York Post* 59cl; Ryan Miller 51fcrb; Photodisc/

Hans Neleman 20cr; Photodisc/Timothy Hughes 20br; Photonica/Cavan Images 14crb; PhotosIndia. com 48c; Adam Pretty 54c; SSPL 64bc; Stone/Daly and Newton 14cra; Stone/Frank Herholdt 15tl; Stone/ Nisian Hughes 39cr, 48cl; Stone/Paul Bradbury 33fcra; Hector Vivas/Jam Media/LatinContent 55tr; Lisa Maree Williams 47tr; Workbook Stock/Paul Giamou 15clb; Jerome Yeats 55cra. **The Kobal Collection:** 20th Century Fox/Merrick Morton 72ca; 20th Century Fox 58cl, 68tr; Walt Disney/Peter Mountain 85tc; Dreamworks/Universal/Jaap Buitendijk 85cra; Lawrence Gordon/Mutual Film/Paramount/Alex Bailey 85cr; New Line/Saul Zaentz/Wing Nut/Pierre Vinet 85bc; Paramount 73clb; Paramount/Stephen Vaughan 85c; Walt Disney Pictures 73c; Warner Bros. 73br. **Rex Features:** 20th Century Fox/Everett 69c, 82; Buena Vista/Everett 81br; Donald Cooper 46cra; Denkou Images 82tr; Kieran Dodds 74br; Everett Collection 25tc, 51tr, 65cb, 73tl; ITV 65c, 72cla; Geraint Lewis 46bc; James D. Morgan 47cla; Alastair Muir 46cl, 47bl, 75tc; New Line/Everett 73bc; New World/ Everett 32–33 (background); Snap 72clb; Startraks Photo 28–29. **TopFoto.co.uk:** 65fbl; Geoff Caddick 39fbl; Francis Loney/Arena PAL 54–55; Colette Masson/Roger-Viollet 50cr; RIA Novosti 81cl; Warner Bros. 81cr; Warner Bros./FotoWare FotoStation/ Topham Picturepoint 85br.

Jacket images: *Back:* **Dreamstime.com:** 350jb tr; Sean Nel ftl. **iStockphoto.com:** Creativeye99 tl.

All other images © Dorling Kindersley
For further information see:

www.dkimages.com